THE BOOK OF

Country Herbal Crafts

by Dawn Cusick

PHOTOGRAPHY BY EVAN BRACKEN

RODALE PRESS
EMMAUS, PENNSYLVANIA

Dedicated in loving memory to
Helen Proctor Duggan
2 June 1897 to 2 February 1945

and to

Nancy McCauley, whose lovely garden crafts
have brought pleasure to so many lives

Published by Rodale Press, Inc.
33 East Minor Street, Emmaus, PA 18098

Produced by Altamont Press, Inc.
50 College Street, Asheville, NC 28801

Editor: Barbara Ellis
Associate Editor: Jean M.A. Nick
Copy Editor: Cheryl Winters-Tetreau
Editorial Assistance: Chris Rich
Art Director: Marcia Winters
Production: Elaine Thompson, Sandra Montgomery
Photography: Evan Bracken, Light Reflections
Photo Art Direction: Diane Weaver
Illustrations: Diane Weaver
Cover Photography: Donna H. Chiarelli
Cover Styling: Dee Schlagel, Design Discovery

For information, write: Rodale Press, Book Reader Service
33 East Minor Street, Emmaus, PA 18098

Printed in the United States of America

Library of Congress Cataloging-in-Publication Data
Cusick, Dawn.
  The book of country herbal crafts : a step-by-step guide to making over
100 beautiful wreaths, garlands, bouquets, and much more / by Dawn Cusick ;
photography by Evan Bracken.
    p.   cm.
  Includes bibliographical references and index.
  ISBN 0-87857-938-9 hardcover
  1. Wreaths.   2. Herbs--Utilization.   3. Flower arrangement.
4. Nature craft.   5. Topiary work.   6. Cookery (Herbs)   I. Title.
SB449.5.W74C87   1991
745.92--dc20   91-10334
                                                     CIP

Distributed in the book trade by St. Martin's Press

2 4 6 8 10 9 7 5 3 1 hardcover

CONTRIBUTING DESIGNERS

Nora Blose, whose aunt was a country doctor and herbalist during the depression, began gardening with herbs as a way to learn about the plants her aunt loved so much. Nora resides in Enka, North Carolina, and markets her herbal crafts under the name "Nora's Follies." (Pages 55, 104, 142, 147, 148, 150, 152, 154, and 171.)

Darlene Conti began growing herbs as a way to landscape the steep mountain land around her home in Asheville, North Carolina. Darlene especially enjoys growing fragrant herbs such as anise and horehound, and uses her talents as a floral designer in her herbal crafts. (Pages 60, 64, 65, 76, 77, 92, 95, 110, 139, and 144.)

Jeannette Hafner grows her craft herbs in her gardens in Orange, Connecticut. She teaches flower and herb drying techniques as well as design classes, and sells her wreaths and arrangements at craft fairs. (Pages 53, 101, 105, 111, 119, 126, and 141.)

Kate Jayne and her husband, Fairman, grow an extensive variety of culinary, decorative, and fragrant herbs at their mountaintop farm, the Sandy Mush Herb Nursery, in Leicester, North Carolina. Kate's wreaths, garlands, and pot-pourris are well known for their natural beauty and fragrance. (Pages 56, 74, 75, 93, 113, 131, 136, 137, and 145.)

Claudette Mautor owns the Yellow Mountain Flower Farm in Leicester, North Carolina, where she grows all of the materials for her crafts. Claudette specializes in projects made from pressed herbs, and enjoys finding new ways to showcase them. Claudette is co-author of *Everlasting Floral Gifts*. (Pages 118, 120-122, and 124.)

Nancy McCauley's floral and herbal needlepoint designs have won international awards and recognition. She enjoys displaying her natural arrangements together with her needle-point, and markets her herbal crafts from her home in Oak Ridge, Tennessee, under the name of "From Grans." (Pages 48, 50, 59, 62, 63, 67, 70, 84, 86, 89, 90, 102, and 133.)

Rob Pulleyn gardens from his home in Asheville, North Carolina. He enjoys cooking for large groups and creating new herb recipes. Rob is author of *The Wreath Book* and co-author of *Everlasting Floral Gifts* and *Wreaths 'Round the Year*. (Pages 156, 158, 160, 162, 164, 166, 168, and 170.)

Susan Thomas, owner of the Pequea Trading Co. in Strasburg, Pennsylvania, enjoys designing wreaths using herbs and dried flowers. Her crafts and materials are pictured on the front cover.

Sylvia Tippett's dream of cultivating an herb farm began when she was an army wife. Every two or three years her husband would be transferred and she would have to say goodbye to a cherished garden. Today she runs Rasland Farms, a family-owned business situated on eight acres in Godwin, North Carolina. (Pages 42, 107, 108, and 149-top.)

Diane Weaver, together with her husband Dick, owns Gourmet Gardens, an herb specialty shop, garden, and greenhouse in Weaverville, North Carolina. Her background in fine art, graphic design, and advertising art direction adds a unique flair to her herbal crafts, and her illustrations accompany the how-to instructions in this book. (Pages 41, 44, 46, 52, 71, 81, 83, 98, 100, 115, 116, 128, and 157.)

Also Thanks to: Corinne Erb (Page 134); Stella Smith (Page 125); basketmaker Jim Hoffmann (Pages 22, 38, 96); James Tate; Herman and Eula Haynes; Claudette Mautor (pages 12–21); and to Bejano's Furnishings in Waynesville, North Carolina; Elkin's Antiques in Weaverville, North Carolina; Gourmet Gardens in Weaverville, North Carolina; Sandy Mush Herb Nursery in Leicester, North Carolina; and Nora Blose in Enka, North Carolina for the generous use of their businesses and gardens for location photography.

CONTENTS

INTRODUCTION

Herbs enjoy a unique and wondrous past, reaching back through countless centuries and civilizations. Ancient cultures viewed herbs as medicinal cure-alls. The early Egyptians used chamomile to cure malarial chills, while the Greeks used feverfew to reduce fevers. *Culpeper's Herbal*, the famous 17th-century reference book that noted herbal tonics and salves, was slowly displaced with the advent of more formalized medicine in the 1800s. In Victorian times, when presenting the illusion of gentility was the personal priority of many, herbs were revered for their pleasing fragrances and symbolic meanings. Today, herbs are enjoying a surge in popularity for their culinary uses.

If humans do share in a collective unconscious, herbs are most certainly a part of it. As a species, we seem determined to keep herbs involved in the day-to-day activities of our lives, and now country crafters are opening our eyes to new uses for herbs beyond the traditional medicinal, fragrance, and culinary functions. After enjoying the lush beauty of their herb gardens, these crafters are drying their herbs and making them into wreaths, garlands, swags, arrangements, topiaries, and many other creative items. Their crafts showcase the true beauty of herbs.

After assembling several books featuring crafts from floral designers, I've noticed many distinct differences in herbal crafters. First, they absolutely cherish their materials. While a florist may get his or her materials delivered to the doorstep twice a week by a wholesaler, herbal crafters almost always grow their materials at home, in their own gardens, often establishing a close relationship with their materials from the germination stage. Floral crafters produce their crafts from materials everyone acknowledges to be inherently beautiful, while herbal crafters often face the common myths that their materials—herbs—are devoid of color, look like weeds and grasses, and are only useful for seasoning foods.

The project designers featured in this book became fascinated with herbs for a variety of reasons. Several designers were long-time floral crafters who discovered how beautifully herbs complemented their work. Other designers were avid herb gardeners searching for a way to transform their hobby into a business. And one designer, whose aunt was a country herbalist in the foothills of Tennessee during the depression, began gardening with herbs as a way to learn about the plants her aunt loved so much.

Although the instructions for each project call for very precise quantities of materials, do not be afraid to add your own "designer touches" to a project. If a garland's instructions call for 50 stems of oregano and your passion is sage, by all means make your garland with sage. If your garden blessed you with an abundance of globe amaranth but refused to yield roses, feel free to substitute.

Best wishes with your gardens and your crafts.

The Herbal Crafter's Garden

People have been trying to define the word herb almost as long as they've been growing them. The definition "anything that has been historically used for medicinal, culinary, or fragrance purposes," has been adopted for classification purposes in this book.

Herbs are one of our most direct connections with ancient civilizations. In 2000 BC, Egypt reputedly had almost 2000 herbal doctors, and foreign interest in the Egyptian invention of embalming, which used herbs in its recipe, stimulated world trade. The medicinal uses of herbs were also researched and documented in the ancient cultures of India, Assyria, Greece, and Rome.

Initially, herb gardens were cultivated simply for medicinal reasons. By AD 830, though, the Romans had escalated gardening to an art form, planting geometrically shaped gardens in their courtyards and embellishing them with potted shrubs, topiaries, and water pools. Herb beds found in the ruins of Moorish-Islamic Spain indicate they gardened as the Romans did, with plants and pools laid out to be enjoyed both in the courtyards and from overlooking windows.

In medieval days, culinary herbs were cultivated as crops. These herbs, including sage, savory, and mustard were used to disguise the unpleasant smells and tastes of rotting meats, and were made into stock by people too poor to afford meats. It wasn't until the Renaissance that gardeners began including several colorful herbs in their gardens purely for their ornamental appeal.

Nineteenth-century Europe saw the birth of English landscape gardens, cottage gardens, and the English flower garden, all of which valued herbs for their aesthetic, fragrant, and medicinal characteristics. Today, herbs are grown for a myriad of reasons, one of the newest being for use in country crafts.

The charts on the following pages provide interesting information on the histories of specific craft herbs, as well as practical information on growing requirements and propagation methods. Most of the craft projects in this book are made from dried herbs, so the charts also include harvesting and drying information. Following the charts are garden layouts designed to provide landscaping ideas for many popular craft herbs. The techniques needed to use them in more than 100 craft projects are described in chapter 2.

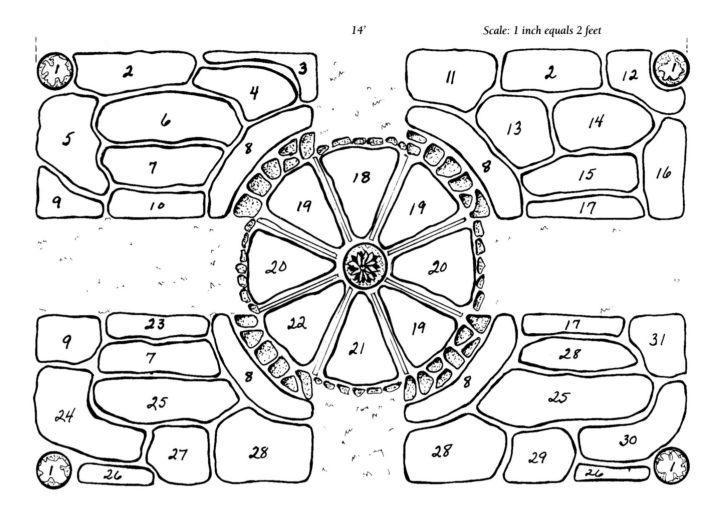

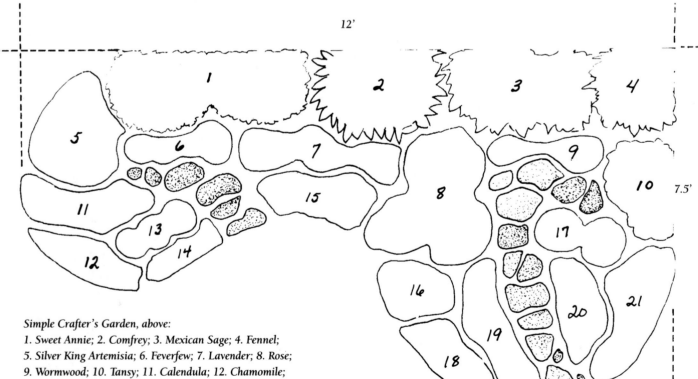

12'

7.5'

Simple Crafter's Garden, above:
1. Sweet Annie; 2. Comfrey; 3. Mexican Sage; 4. Fennel;
5. Silver King Artemisia; 6. Feverfew; 7. Lavender; 8. Rose;
9. Wormwood; 10. Tansy; 11. Calendula; 12. Chamomile;
13. Chive; 14. Thyme; 15. Heather; 16. Sage; 17. Anise Hyssop;
18. Oregano; 19. Lamb's Ear; 20. Dusty Miller; 21. Dianthus.

Scale: 1 inch equals 2 feet

Gardens have been enchanting their caretakers for centuries, and your herbal craft garden will undoubtedly do the same for you. Your garden can be as formal or casual as you like, and the layouts shown here were designed to inspire you. But keep in mind that herbs grow just as well in rows in your vegetable garden, or mixed with flowers in your borders. The herbs in these gardens were chosen because of their compatibility (they require similar amounts of sun and water) and their ability to dry well for use in crafts. Before laying out your own garden, spend some time perusing the craft projects in this book. Take note of the materials in your favorite projects, and adjust their representation in your garden accordingly.

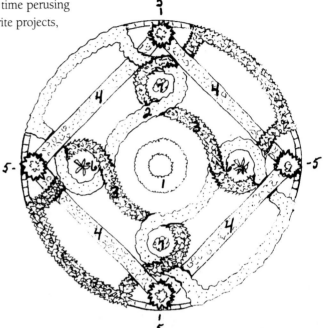

The Knot Garden, right:
1. Grey Santolina; 2. Green Santolina; 3. Lavender Munstead;
4. Germander; 5. Rosemary; 6. Tansy; 7. Mealy Cup Sage.

Country Crafter's Garden, opposite page, top:
1. Geranium; 2. Pearly Everlasting; 3. Marjoram; 4. Calendula;
5. Cornflower; 6. Sweet Annie; 7. Globe Amaranth; 8. Blue Salvia;
9. Chamomile; 10. Tarragon; 11. Oregano; 12. Silver Germander;
13. Silver King Artemisia; 14. Yarrow; 15. Lavender; 16. Wormwood;
17. Santolina; 18. Cockscomb; 19. Mint; 20. Thyme; 21. Bee Balm;
22. Lemon Balm; 23. Chives; 24. Anise Hyssop; 25. Strawflower;
26. Lamb's Ear; 27. Tansy; 28. Mexican Sage; 29. Feverew;
30. Heather; 31. Dusty Miller.

HERBS

Common/ Botanical Name	History	Method of Propagation
Anise Hyssop *Agastache foeniculum*	Anise hyssop was once called "Licorice mint."	Seeds, cuttings
Basil, Sweet *Ocimum basilicum*	As a member of the mint family, basil has a reputation for curing stomach ills. In India, basil leaves placed on the breasts of the dead served as guaranteed passports to paradise. Elsewhere in the world, basil was actually feared.	Seeds
Bee Balm *Monarda didyma*	Bee balm, also known as Oswego tea and bergamot, has a lovely, citrus fragrance. Bees are said to find their way home by tracking the smell of this herb.	Cuttings, seeds, division
Blue Salvia *Salvia azurea*	Also known as blue sage, blue salvia is a half-hardy, late-blooming perennial treasured for its tiny, blue to white flowers, which bloom in clustered spikes along its gray-haired stems. The herb is sometimes found in bogs or along brooks.	Seeds, cuttings, division
Calendula *Calendula officinalis*	Summer's bride, as it was once called, came to America with the earliest settlers. This bright yellow- to orange-colored marigold plays a prominent role in folklore. Its presence in a pocket guaranteed courtroom justice, while its presence in a bedroom promised love.	Seeds
Carnation *Dianthus* spp.	Carnations, also known as gilliflowers, were used in wine recipes and were once believed to give strength to the ailing. They are still included in get-well bouquets and their delicate aroma is supposed to relieve headaches.	Seeds, cuttings
Catnip *Nepeta cataria*	Catnip is not only a mild and harmless aphrodisiac for cats, but repels rodents as well. Farmers once protected their homes and outbuildings from rats by surrounding the structures with catnip plants.	Seeds
Chamomile *Matricaria recutita, M.eximia,* and *Chamaemelum nobile*	Chamomile was known as the plant's physician because its presence was believed to strengthen and protect plants growing nearby. When lawns were first cultivated, chamomile was chosen as a groundcover because it spread easily and released a fruity fragrance when crushed.	Seeds, cuttings
Chives *Allium schoenoprasum*	Chives belong to the Allium family, along with onions and garlic. Their strong flavor and fragrance, valued as culinary additions, are also reputed to keep evil spirits, illnesses, and even the elements at bay.	Seeds, division of bulbs
Cockscomb *Celosia cristata*	Cockscomb derives its common name from the somewhat peculiar shapes formed by its tiny, clustered flowers. The flowers range in color from red to bronze to gold and earned the plant its Greek name *celosia,* meaning burnt.	Seeds
Comfrey *Symphytum officinale*	Also known as knit back or healing herb, comfrey has been used to treat wounds and to mend broken bones since the days of ancient Greece. Comfrey also protects those who carry it when they travel.	Seeds, root division, cuttings

Growing Requirements	Parts Used	Harvesting Information
Full sun; average, well-drained soil	Flowers, seed heads	Both anise hyssop's fragrant lavender flowers and its light brown pods are attractive in herbal crafts. Harvest the flowers when they are two-thirds mature; harvest the pods when the seeds are mature.
Full sun to partial shade; average, well-drained soil	Flowers, leaves	Dry basil is fragile and loses its fragrance rapidly, but can be used in flower arrangements and potpourris. Live basil serves well as a protective companion plant in the garden.
Full sun to shade; average, well-drained soil	Flowers, seed heads	In order to preserve their brilliant colors, harvest bee balm flowers early in the bloom cycle. Harvest the seed heads after the blooms have died and before the first frost.
Full sun; partial shade; average, well-drained soil	Flowers	Blue salvia should be hung to dry in small bunches and handled gently to prevent breakage.
Full sun; average, well-drained soil	Flowers	Harvest calendula when the blossoms are fully opened. To dry, arrange short-stemmed flowers face down on a screen. Flowers may also be dried in the microwave.
Full sun; average, well-drained soil	Flowers	Both single and double carnation blossoms can be cut and dried, whether in bud or open, although open flowers will take considerable time to dry thoroughly. Microwaving works well.
Full sun to partial shade; average to moist, well-drained soil	Flowers, leaves	This hardy perennial grows quickly, so up to three cuttings can be taken each season. Be sure to leave some plants undisturbed when making second and third cuttings so they will reseed. Hang or stand plants out of direct sunlight to dry.
Full sun; average, well-drained soil	Flowers, leaves	Harvest the leaves for potpourri when they are 1 to 2 inches (2-1/2 to 5 cm.) long. The short-stemmed flowers should be harvested when they are in full bloom, and they can be dried on a cloth or screen.
Full sun; average, well-drained soil	Flowers	Chives' pale pink and lavender flowers cluster in globe-shaped flower heads. Their color will hold well if the heads are harvested when fully open and either dried on a screen or hung.
Full sun; average, well-drained soil	Flowers	Unlike most flowers, cockscomb should be cut when the blossoms are dew-covered to prevent matting. Cut in late summer, before the blossoms have opened completely, and remove foliage to speed drying. Place upright in a vase for three days in a dark, well-ventilated room and then hang in small bunches.
Full sun to partial shade; average, well-drained soil	Leaves	Harvest comfrey's leaves during the summer months and dry them on screens.

Common/ Botanical Name	History	Method of Propagation
Dill *Anethum graveolens*	This easily grown pot herb, long valued for its flavor, was once a part of ships' provisions because sailors believed it prevented disease. It is still a popular culinary herb, and its oils are used in soap making.	Seeds
Dusty Miller *Artemisia stellerana*	Dusty miller takes its common name from the white, woolly hairs covering its leaves. Also known as old woman, these perennials were planted by the entrances to homes to represent elderly residents.	Seeds, cuttings, division
Fennel *Foeniculum vulgare*	Biennial fennel is tall and graceful, and is reputed to afford magical protective properties to those who carry or wear it. Fragrant and licorice-tasting, the greenery is often tinged bronze. Fennel is an attractive addition to any garden, and was grown by the Cherokee Indians for use in the treatment of colic and colds.	Seeds
Feverfew *Chrysanthemum parthenium*	Also called featherfew, this herb was valued for its healing and protective powers, and was also used to drive away unwelcome bees.	Seeds, division, cuttings
Geranium, Scented *Pelargonium* spp	Reportedly, where geraniums grow the snakes will not go. Flowering pink geraniums were once used in love potions.	Cuttings
Goldenrod *Solidago* spp	The most popular of the goldenrods, sweet-scented *Solidago odora*, or blue mountain tea, used to bring high market prices as an import to Britain until it was discovered growing by the wayside. The herb's long history as a wound healer is reflected in its Latin name, which means to unite.	Cuttings, seeds
Heather *Calluna vulgaris*	Like so many of the plants that arrived from across the Atlantic, heather was thought to bring good luck. Common in arid locations, heather was also believed to bring rain.	Cuttings
Horehound *Marrubium vulgare*	Called "eye of the star" by Egyptian priests and named for the Egyptian god Horus, horehound was esteemed as a cure for many ills.	Seeds
Italian Oregano *Origanum vulgare*	Also known as pot marjoram and winter or wild oregano, Italian oregano is native to the Mediterranean. This hardy, perennial plant has been used medicinally for centuries to treat a wide variety of ailments. As a dye, the flowers turn linens reddish-brown and wools a deep purple.	Cuttings, seeds
Korean Mint *Agastache rugosa*	This little-known perennial herb was once used by Jews as a strewing herb. The leaves have been enjoyed in teas for their spearmint flavor.	Seeds
Lamb's Ear *Stachys byzantina*	Sometimes called wooly betony, this furry, white-leafed perennial is no longer used as it once was, to bandage wounds, but its beauty makes it a welcome addition to the garden. The tall, flowering plant attracts bees and butterflies, which hover over its tiny lavender blossoms from dawn till dusk.	Seeds

Growing Requirements	Parts Used	Harvesting Information
Full sun; average, well-drained soil	Flowers	Dill's pale yellow flowers open in clusters on its airy stems. Cut for drying when three-quarters of the clusters are open. To dry, stand or hang in a dark, moisture-free environment.
Full sun; dry, well-drained soil	Leaves	Dusty miller's foliage can be dried by placing individual leaves on a drying rack.
Sun to partial shade; average to moist, well-drained soil	Flowers	Harvest fennel's flowers when the pollen is still present. The large, pale yellow flowers are fragile but dry well. Lay them face down on a screen or hang loosely in small bundles.
Full sun; average, well-drained soil	Flowers	Feverfew blooms in late summer, and after cutting it will continue to produce flowers until the first frost. Harvest the flowers just before they mature. The flowers dry well when hung in small handfuls and can also be microwaved.
Full sun; average, well-drained soil	Leaves	When dried, geraniums hold their fragrance better than they retain their color. Harvest the fresh leaves carefully, one at a time, and lay them on a screen to dry. Some leaves will dry to a light green color, some to a silver gray, and others to a light, golden brown.
Full sun to partial shade; dry to average, well-drained soil	Flowers, leaves	Harvest the flowers for arrangements when half open; hang or stand to dry.
Sun to partial shade; dry to average, well-drained soil	Flowers, stems, sprigs	Heathers bloom in shades of white to pink to pale purple, and have narrow single or double blooms. Harvest when half to three-fourths of the flowers are open. Dry on a screen or in the microwave, since the flowers are delicate. The foliage, which changes color in the fall and winter, can be harvested anytime and will retain its colors well.
Full sun; average, well-drained soil	Seed heads, leaves	Harvest the leaves and seed heads before they turn brown. Lay them on a cloth or screen to dry.
Full sun; average, well-drained soil	Leaves, flowers	Harvest the leaves for drying as soon as the flowers have appeared. Unlike the leaves of many other herbs, oregano leaves may be dried in direct sunlight.
Partial sun; average, well-drained soil	Flowers	To dry, strip the leaves from the stems and hang to dry.
Full sun to partial shade; dry to average, well-drained soil	Flowers, leaves	Arrangers who work with naturals use lamb's ear year-round. The herb is easy to grow, rarely harmed by insects, and lasts for years once dried. Cut stems, flower stalks, or individual dew-free leaves before the frost and hang to dry.

Common/ Botanical Name	History	Method of Propagation
Lavender *Lavandula angustifolia*	In Roman times, lavender was quite expensive because it was believed that a dangerous breed of snake called the asp lived under lavender shrubs. Ironically, lavender was also thought to provide protection against physical ailments. Today, lavender is valued for its fragrance and is a common ingredient in sachets and soaps.	Cuttings, seeds
Lavender Cotton *Santolina chamaecyparissus*	Santolina probably got its common name; lavender cotton, because its small leaves look like fuzzy lavender leaves. A very fragrant herb, santolina is highly valued as an insect repellent.	Seeds, cuttings
Lemon Balm *Melissa officinalis*	Both people and animals love the citrus smell of lemon balm's leaves. Beehives rubbed with lemon balm will attract and keep bees.	Seeds
Marguerite *Chrysanthemum frutescens*	Originally from the Canary Islands, marguerites were brought to France during the late 16th century and are sometimes called Paris daisies. Roots placed under pillows are reputed to bring pleasant dreams.	Seeds, cuttings, division
Mealy-Cup Sage *Salvia farinacea*	Mealy-cup sage is named for the cuplike calyxes from which its violet-blue petals emerge. Its fragrant flowers, gray-green leaves, and fuzzy gray stems make lovely additions to arrangements.	Seeds, division
Mint *Mentha* spp.	In the 15th century, mint was taken to settle the stomach and was administered as a cure for worms. In potions of all sorts, it symbolized health, wealth, and travel.	Cuttings, division
Mountain Mint *Pycnanthemum* spp.	Mountain mint is a hardy, aromatic perennial that grows well in the wild. Its flowers range from pink to white and bloom in mid-summer. Bees favor the nectar from these densely clustered blossoms and produce a rich honey from them.	Seeds, cuttings, division
Oregano *Origanum* spp.	Many species of oregano exist, and many have long histories as medicinals. The Greeks named wild marjoram, one species of oregano, *oros ganos,* or joy of the mountain.	Cuttings, seeds
Parsley *Petroselinum crispum*	Ancient Romans cast parsley upon the water of fish ponds to cure unhealthy fish, and the Greeks wove this herb into the wreaths they bestowed upon victorious athletes.	Seeds
Pennyroyal *Mentha pulegium* and *Hedeoma pulegioides*	Pennyroyal, once known as the herb of peace and lurk-in-the-ditch, was used to remove spells and to end fights. Soldiers carried pennyroyal to war with them.	Seeds, cuttings
Purple Coneflower *Echinacea angustifolia*	This tall, native American plant has a long medicinal history. American Indians used purple coneflowers to strengthen their magic spells.	Seeds, division

H E R B S

Growing Requirements	Parts Used	Harvesting Information
Full sun; average, well-drained soil	Flowers, stems, leaves	Lavender's flowers, stems, and leaves all remain fragrant after drying. Harvest the flowers for arrangements when they are three-fourths open. Those for use in potpourris and sachets can be harvested during their active growing season and before the first frost.
Full sun; average, well-drained soil	Flowers	Santolina's lemon yellow flowers hold their color best when harvested just before full bloom. Though small, the flowers are dense and will take some time to dry. The fragile foliage should be harvested in the fall and hung to dry with care. Dried santolina is excellent in potpourri; it has a lovely scent and is easily crushed.
Full sun; average, well-drained soil	Flowers, leaves	Lemon balm's aroma remains after drying. Leaves for potpourri should be gathered late in the growing season before they become tough and before the first frost. Cut the plants just above ground level.
Partial sun; average, well-drained soil	Flowers, leaves	Dry the flowers and foliage in a moisture-absorbing desiccant such as sand or silica gel.
Full sun to partial shade; average, well-drained soil	Leaves, flowers, stems	Harvest the flowers before they have opened completely, and hang to dry with the leaves intact.
Full sun to partial shade; average to moist, well-drained soil	Flowers, leaves, sprigs	Flowers for arrangements should be picked when nearly mature and dried by hanging. The leaves may be picked at any green stage of growth and should be stripped from stems before screen drying. The leaves and flowers may also be dried in the microwave.
Partial shade; average, well-drained soil	Flowers	Hang to dry in small bundles in a dark, dry area.
Full sun; average, well-drained soil	Flowers, leaves, sprigs	Oregano, whether fresh or dry, is fragrant and airy in shape. Most of oregano's color resides in its bracts, so harvest them before the last of the tiny flowers has faded. Harvest the stems and leaves for fragrance. The stems are thin and should be spread or stood carefully for drying.
Full sun; average, well-drained soil	Flowers, leaves	Parsley flowers and leaves dry well in the microwave but should be dried separately. For potpourris, the plants can be hung to dry. Remove dried leaves from the stems and chop or crumble to size.
Full sun to partial shade; average, well-drained soil	Leaves	The runners should be snipped to release them from the ground. The runners dry quickly and, although they are tiny, act as effective pest repellents when added to potpourri.
Full sun to partial shade; dry to average, well-drained soil	Flowers	Cut the stems of this tall plant before the flower centers have elongated. The flowers will dry dark brown to black if harvested after their centers have crowned.

H E R B S

Common/ Botanical Name	History	Method of Propagation
Queen Anne's Lace *Daucus carota*	Just when this kin to the carrot was first discovered is unknown, but its roots have been added to stews for centuries. The Cherokee Indians used Queen Anne's lace in baths to reduce swelling, and the delicate plants have served as inspiration for countless filigree and lace designs.	Seeds
Rose *Rosa* spp.	In ancient legends, the rose was known as Cupid's flower, and was said to grow best when stolen. The petals, sprinkled around the home, are said to contribute to internal harmony.	Cuttings
Rosemary *Rosmarinus officinalis*	Rosemary — a symbol of love, loyalty, and remembrance — has been a traditional gift for wedding guests and for friends at the New Year.	Cuttings
Safflower *Carthamus tinctorius*	Also known as American saffron, dyer's saffron, and Mexican saffron, this hardy annual's flowers render potent dyes that are used to color foods, cosmetics, leathers, and textiles. The Egyptians wore safflower flowers in necklaces.	Seeds
Sage *Salvia officinalis* (or) spp.	In French sage means wisdom, and the Latin term salvia means salvation. Since the days of ancient Rome, sage has been cultivated for its ability to strengthen the mind and increase longevity.	Seeds, cuttings
Salad Burnet *Poterium sanguisorba*	Sir Francis Bacon, in his famous essay *Of Gardens,* recommended that salad burnet be planted in walkways so that its cucumber-like fragrance would be released as it was crushed. Its leaves were thought to protect against the plague and to cure rheumatism and gout.	Seeds, division
Silver King Artemisia *Artemisia ludoviciana var. albula*	Silver king artemisia is a stunning ornamental herb, the foliage of which is covered with fine, white hairs. Also called the ghost plant, its leaves make lovely additions to winter bouquets.	Seeds, cuttings
Sweet Annie *Artemisia annua*	Also known as sweet wormwood, this fragrant herb was once made into small bouquets by European housekeepers and brushed over clothing.	Cuttings, root division
Sweet Bay *Laurus nobilis*	Thousands of years ago bay was used by Delphic priestesses as protection against evil. Roman poets and heroes wore wreaths of laurel berries, and the term baccalaureate derived its name from this ancient use of bay.	Cuttings
Tansy *Tanacetum vulgare*	Tansy derives its name from *athanasia,* the Greek word for immortality. Used in Finland as a dye plant and in medieval England as a stewing herb, tansy's strong fragrance and color have made it a favorite in many gardens.	Seeds, division, cuttings
Tarragon, French *Artemisia dracunculus*	The domestic tarragon of today is similar to the wild artemisias grown during the 16th century. Its primary uses are in cooking and perfumery.	Cuttings

Growing Requirements	Parts Used	Harvesting Information
Full sun; average, well-drained soil	Flowers, seed heads	Queen Anne's lace may be harvested before the flowers are fully open and dried in glycerin, or cut after the flowers are open and hung. For an airy, wintery look, harvest after the seed heads are mature.
Full sun to partial shade; average, well-drained soil	Flowers, rose hips	These lovely blossoms are slow to dry and should be harvested before they are fully open. Hanging, microwaving, and desiccant drying all work well, but do give them ample time to dry. Gather dry rose hips before frost, or before they begin to wither on the bush.
Full sun to partial shade; average, well-drained soil	Leaves	Harvest rosemary when the plant is fully mature, because the young growth will shrivel and turn black. Dry by laying the branches on a screen. Dried rosemary leaves are very fragrant, but tend to turn dark brown and fall from their stems.
Full sun; dry, well-drained soil	Flowers, seed heads	Hang flowers and seed heads upside down in a dark, well-ventilated area.
Full sun to partial shade; average, well-drained soil	Leaves, flowers	Many variations of sage exist. The leaves of most varieties retain their fragrance well and should be harvested as soon as, or just before, they mature. Remove the leaves from cut stems and spread on a screen to dry. The flowers dry better when hung and should be cut when they are young.
Full sun; average, well-drained soil	Leaves, seeds	Salad burnet remains colorful almost year-round and can be harvested for drying until the first snowfall. Hang to dry. For best color retention, dry quickly in a hot, shaded area.
Full sun; average, well-drained soil	Leaves	Silver king artemisia may be harvested twice: once for the foliage, before the seed heads have developed, when the leaves are white and lacy; and the second time for its brown seeds, when the foliage feels and looks like wool. Hang upside down to dry if straight lines are desired; dry upright in a vase if curved lines are desired.
Full sun; average, well-drained soil	Flowers, leaves, sprigs	Sweet Annie's wonderful fragrance and wispy texture make it a favorite material for wreaths and arrangements. Hang by drying in small bundles upside down.
Full sun to shade; average, well-drained soil	Leaves	Harvest the leaves separately or cut stems when they are mature. Dry bay should be stored away from light in closed containers.
Full sun to partial shade; average, well-drained soil	Flowers, leaves	Harvest the flower heads in late summer when their green color has changed to a deep, golden yellow. Hang in a protected area of the house to avoid attracting flies. Strip the leaves from the stems for best results and dry in a well-ventilated area.
Full sun; average, well-drained soil	Flowers, leaves, sprigs	Tarragon's delicate flowers are attractive in vinegars and salads, but rarely hold when dried. Harvest the leaves before it flowers.

Common/ Botanical Name	History	Method of Propagation
Baby's-Breath *Gypsophila* spp.	In spite of its delicate appearance and name, baby's-breath grows in the harsh climates of Romania, Turkey, and Siberia. Also known as flower fountain and wispy blossom bush, it is a favorite of florists and brides.	Seeds
Bachelor's Button *Centaurea cyanus*	Love is reputed to come to those who wear or carry this blossom, in spite of its folk name, Devil's flower. Its everlasting freshness and royal hue make the flower popular in crafts.	Seeds
Black-Eyed Susan *Rudbeckia hirta*	Also known as coneflowers and yellow daisies, black-eyed Susans bloom profusely in midsummer, often in open fields where livestock fortunately shun them.	Seeds
Curry Plant *Helichrysum angustifolium*	Most of the flowers in this genus make wonderful everlastings and their fragrance is reminiscent of the spices used in curry.	Seeds, cuttings
Globe Amaranth *Gomphrena globosa*	This popular everlasting was a favorite addition to bouquets and nosegays at the turn of the century.	Seeds
Job's Tears *Coix lacryma-jobi*	Job's tears, an ornamental grass native to India and China, is named for its tear-shaped seeds. These lustrous, pearly-gray seeds are often strung into necklaces and rosaries.	Seeds
Larkspur *Delphinium hybridum*	Shakespeare called this plant lark's heel, and others have known it as lark's toe or knight's spur. The flower is reported to keep ghosts at bay.	Seeds
Love-In-A-Mist *Nigella damascena*	The seeds of nigella have flavored baked goods in Egypt for centuries. Nigella derives its Latin name from Damascus, the city from which it was exported during the 16th century.	Seeds
Pearly Everlasting *Anaphalis margaritacea*	Everlastings have long symbolized romantic love. Pure in color and enduring in quality, their white blossoms often appeared in Victorian bouquets. Also known as chafe weed, Indian posy, and old field balsam, everlastings have historically been used in spells to restore youth.	Seeds, division
Statice (Annual, Caspia, German) *Limonium* spp.	A common name for several of the purple-flowering statices is sea lavender. These plants grow near to and smell like the sea, and their tiny, purple flowers resemble those of lavender.	Seeds
Strawflower *Helichrysum bracteatum*	Native to Crete and Asia Minor, colorful strawflowers make lovely everlastings and are a favorite of crafters.	Seeds
Sweet gum *Liquidambar styraciflua*	The sweet gum, a deciduous tree, is valued for its brilliant fall colors, its hard wood, and its medicinal qualities.	Seeds, cuttings, grafting

Growing Requirements	Parts Used	Harvesting Information
Full sun; average, well-drained soil	Flowers	Baby's-breath tends to tangle as it grows, so clip the stems and separate them carefully. Hang in loose bundles because the threadlike stems are fragile.
Full sun; dry to average, well-drained soil	Flowers	The flowers should be collected either at the bud stage or when fully open but before they begin to age. To dry, hang or microwave.
Full sun; average, well-drained soil	Flowers	Dry the flowers face-up in a moisture-absorbing desiccant for approximately two weeks or hang upside down.
Full sun; average, well-drained soil	Flowers	Harvest before the blossoms are fully opened and hang in small, loose bundles to dry. Be careful not to crack the slender stems near the flower heads.
Full sun; dry to average, well-drained soil	Flowers	Globe amaranth feels dry even when it is fresh. Drying in the microwave is a quick way to make the stems rigid for immediate use. Hanging also works well.
Full sun; average, well-drained soil	Seeds	Harvest the seeds when they reach the desired color and dry on a screen, rotating every few days.
Full sun to partial shade; average, well-drained soil	Flowers	Harvest larkspur when most of the flowers on the stalk have opened. To dry, either microwave or stand flowers in a vase with a little water until the water has evaporated.
Full sun to partial shade; average, well-drained soil	Seed heads	Harvest the seed heads before the first frost when they are fully mature but still green. The heads and stems are very fragile, so hang them in loose bundles to dry.
Full sun; average, well-drained soil	Flowers	Harvest the flowers before their yellow centers have become visible. Cut them on short stems so the side shoots will continue to develop on the plant that remains. Hang, place on screens, or microwave to dry.
Full sun; average, well-drained soil	Flowers	The tiny flowers fall away during drying, leaving the white or colored bracts that are so popular in crafts. In order to keep the colors from fading, harvest the flowers while they are still blooming. Prevent mildewing by hanging the flowers in bunches during hot, dry weather.
Full sun; average, well-drained soil	Flowers	Strawflowers may be harvested from bud stage until their centers begin to show. Their bright colors hold well, but the stems become very weak during the drying process.
Full sun; average, well-drained soil	Seed balls	Harvest in the fall after the seed balls have dropped from the tree.

HARVESTING FRESH HERBS

If you've never harvested herbs before, cutting a large quantity of your most precious garden treasures will be an intimidating experience. Try reminding yourself, though, that almost everything you cut will be enjoyed in a wreath or other project for years to come instead of dying at the end of the garden season.

Bring a large basket or other container with you for harvesting. As you cut, alternate the direction you lay stems and blooms to prevent delicate leaves and petals from crushing each other. Avoid harvesting your herbs when they are damp from morning dew or a recent rain or when above-average temperatures have wilted blooms and foliage.

Other harvesting tips to remember: leave at least 2 inches (5 cm.) of stem when you cut — 6 to 12 inches (15 to 30 cm.) is preferable; if possible, harvest several stems of each herb in different stages of bloom; avoid harvesting herbs with insect damage; try to harvest at least ten percent more than a project's materials list calls for, to allow for breakage.

AIR-DRYING

You may be surprised to learn that many of the herbs in your garden will dry perfectly, with little or no supervision, when simply exposed to air. Air-drying, as this process is called, only requires a warm, dark location with as little humidity as possible. The warm, dry air encourages the natural moisture in the herbs to evaporate, while the darkness prevents the herbs' colors from fading. There are two basic methods of air-drying herbs: hanging and screen drying.

To dry your herbs with the hanging method, simply combine six or more stems in a bundle, secure the stems, and hang upside down. The stems can be secured with string, rubber bands, or even clothes clips. Allow plenty of space between hanging bundles to encourage good air circulation.

Check on the progress of your hanging herbs often. The changes you observe in shape, size, and color will surprise you and give you a good education on the drying process. Some changes are dramatic, others are barely noticeable. Look for buds that may or may not open. What happens to the leaves? If you notice herbs with mildew or insect damage, remove them quickly to prevent the damage from spreading.

Drying times for herbs range from four days to as long as three weeks. Test for dryness by touching the flowers. If they're dry and rigid, they're ready.

Bundles should make a soft rustling sound when gently shaken. Remove the herbs to a cool, moisture-free location when they're dry. Overdrying will make the herbs too brittle to use in crafts.

Herbs can also be air-dried on a wire mesh screen. This method works especially well with materials such as chives, whose blooms will droop if dried upside down, and leaves, that do not have long or strong enough stems to gather in bundles. To prepare the herbs for screen drying, simply strip their stems of leaves and drop them through the holes until the flower blooms rest on the screen. Allow enough space around each bloom or leaf for good air circulation.

Opposite page: Bundles of dried herbs can be tied with colorful raffia and then displayed to add country charm to any room.
Bottom left: To dry blossoms on a screen, simply drop their stems through the wire mesh. Lay individual leaves flat.

Bottom right: This small folding herb drying rack (about 18 inches, 46 cm. tall) can be made as a weekend woodworking project.

GLYCERIN PRESERVING

Many varieties of herbs can be preserved with glycerin. Begin by making several diagonal slices in the lower portions of the stems. Prepare a mixture of three parts warm water to one part glycerin and stand the stems in it for about two weeks. The glycerin is gradually absorbed through the slits in the stems.

DESICCANT DRYING

These moisture-absorbing substances have been used for centuries, and allow you to dry many herbs that cannot be dried with other methods. (If you live in an extremely humid climate, however, drying with desiccants is probably not a good idea because the herbs will re-absorb moisture.) The traditionally used desiccants—sand, borax, and corn-

meal—work well and are inexpensive, but the heavy weight of their crystals can crush delicate materials. Silica gel is more expensive than other desiccants, but its granules are light enough to not cause damage. If you choose to use silica gel, please read and take note of the manufacturer's warnings on the package.

To dry your herbs, simply prepare a plastic or glass container (wood and cardboard containers can allow moisture in) with about an inch (2-1/2 cm.) of desiccant. Place bell- and cup-shaped blooms on their sides, and other blooms face-up, with generous spacing in between. Gently cover the herbs with a layer of desiccant, taking care not to flatten their petals into unnatural positions. The herbs can be layered two or three rows deep, but you shouldn't mix

different types of herbs unless you know their drying times are the same.

Some herbs will dry in three or four days, while others will need as long as a week to ten days. When removing herbs from the desiccant, use a small paintbrush to gently whisk off any left-over powder residue.

MICROWAVE OVEN DRYING

When used with silica gel, microwave drying produces beautiful results in just minutes. Moisture in the herbs is removed during the cooking process and absorbed by the silica gel crystals.

To dry herbs in your microwave you will need a non-metal container and silica gel. Begin by covering the bottom of the container with a thin layer of silica gel. Arrange the herbs as directed in the

Left: With a little practice and experimenting, anyone can dry herbs in a microwave oven with beautiful results.

desiccant drying section. Sprinkle silica gel between the herbs and then add a thin layer on top. A microwave with settings from one through ten should be put on setting number four (about 300 watts); a microwave with three or four settings should be put on "half" (about 350 watts); and a microwave with only "high" and "defrost" settings should be put on "defrost" (200 watts).

The variation in microwaves and in the amount of moisture in a particular herb makes it virtually impossible to predict the exact amount of cooking time necessary. The drying time for one or more blooms or foliage in about half a pound (300 kg) of silica gel is two to two and a half minutes.

After cooking in the microwave, your herbs will need "standing time."

For fragile blooms with only a few petals, the time is usually about ten minutes. Sturdy, heavy-petaled blooms can need up to 30 minutes. To prevent moisture from forming—and being reabsorbed into your herbs—place a top on the container and leave it cracked just a bit. If your herbs are not dry enough after their standing time, they can be microwaved again.

Harvest enough herbs to allow experimentation, and be sure to record your microwave's setting and cooking time each time you achieve perfect results.

PRESSING

Another simple way to dry herbs is by pressing them. Collections of plants dried with this method over 400 years ago are still in good condition today. Prepare your herbs for pressing by separating foliage from flowers. Arrange them on a sheet of blotting paper so that none of the materials are overlapping or creased. Cover them with another sheet of blotting paper and place between the pages of a thick book or in a flower press. The drying process takes anywhere from six to ten weeks to complete.

Below left: Silica gel and other moisture-absorbing desiccants provide a quick way to dry herbs.

Below right: Wooden herb presses are simple to use, and the pressed leaves and blossoms make lovely additions to wall hangings and small gifts.

THE HERBAL CRAFTER'S WORKSHOP

The herbal crafter's workshop is a glorious potpourri of beautiful materials. And whether your own workshop is an entire room or simply a nook under a staircase, you may become so enamored with this work-in-progress look that you'll decide to make it a part of your permanent decor.

In this chapter you will be introduced to the techniques and materials needed to make the projects in this book: lengthening and preparing stems; creating mini bouquets; working with bases, hot glue, wire, and floral tapes; choosing complementary materials; discovering accents; and making bows.

CHOOSING HERBS

Anyone who gardens takes pleasure in watching the subtle developments in the growth of their plants. Some plants even seem to develop personalities that endear them to their grower. Thus it's difficult for many herbal crafters to realize that not every herb is right for every craft project. Choosing the herbs for a specific project involves a myriad of technical and aesthetic considerations. The technical considerations are easy to deal with: Is this herb's stem strong enough to work with? Can it be lengthened? And so on. The answers are generally yes or no and the problem can either be fixed or it cannot.

The aesthetic considerations, however, are a bit more complicated. Professional designers consider the color, texture, shape, and fragrance of each type of herb before choosing it for a project, and these considerations often seem subjective to a beginning crafter. When considering color, for example, strive for subtle blends or strong contrasts. A brilliant magenta bee balm blossom will look all the more brilliant when placed against a dark green background of bay leaves or a neutral background of artemisia. Herbs with interesting textures and shapes should be included to keep the eye's attention. Fragrant herbs such as lavender and sweet Annie add another level of interest to the project.

PREPARING HERBS

Analyzing Stem Strength. The natural strength of a dried herb's stem varies significantly from species to species. The stems of some herbs, such as yarrow, are strong enough to insert directly into floral foam; while the stems of other herbs, such as calendula, are extremely weak. Stems of the same herb from the same garden can also have considerable variation in strength, depending on what stage of growth they were in when harvested and how they were dried.

Before beginning a specific project in this book, read the instructions to find out how the herb materials are used. If the herbs will be attached to floral picks, you do not need to worry about stem strength because the wooden pick will serve as a stem.

If the herbs will be inserted directly into floral foam, however, you will need to prepare your stems before working on the project.

With your fingers near the end of the stem, insert the stem of each herb into a

From bright yellow yarrow to brilliant magenta globe amaranth, herbs come in a beautiful spectrum of colors.

small block of floral foam as a test. If the stem does not break then it is classified as "strong." The only preparation necessary for a strong stem is that it be cut at an angle (see illustration A) to make insertion into the foam easier.

If a sample herb's stem does break when you're trying to insert it into the foam, then the stem is classified as "weak." Weak stems will need to be reinforced with floral wire before using them in a project.

Analyzing Stem Length. Before beginning a project you will also need to compare the length of your stems to the lengths called for in the instructions. If your stems are too long, simply trim them to the called-for length. If they are too short, however, you will need to increase the stems' lengths with floral wire. (Note: Lengthening a stem with floral wire involves the same process as strengthening a stem.)

ADDING STRENGTH OR LENGTH TO A STEM WITH FLORAL WIRE

First examine the existing stem. If the stem is hollow or virtually nonexistent, cut a length of floral wire an inch (2.5 cm.) longer than the length you need the new stem to be. Firmly hold the flower with one hand and gently push one end of the wire up through the stem and the flower head. Bend the protruding wire end into a u-shaped hook (see illustration B), and then pull the hook down until it embeds in the flower head. This new stem can be wrapped with floral tape if you wish to hide the wire or inserted directly into floral foam.

If the existing stem is very weak, position a length of floral wire (cut to the needed length) next to the natural stem so it overlaps about 2 inches (5 cm.). Secure them together with floral tape. (See illustration C.)

A DICTIONARY OF CRAFT TOOLS

Floral Picks are short wooden picks with a tapered point and a short piece of fine-gauge wire attached to one end. Multiple or single stems of herbs and flowers are positioned against the wooden pick, secured with the wire, and then inserted into a foam or straw base. The picks are available in green, brown, and unfinished wood; choose the color that best complements your herb materials.

Floral Pins are small metal pins that resemble old-fashioned hair pins. Floral pins are used to attach moss, herbs, and even lace to foam bases.

Floral Tape is a thin, stretchy, and slightly adhesive tape that's sold in varying shades of green and brown to match herbs and flowers. The tape is used to secure small bouquets together at their stems and to disguise unsightly wire or foam.

Floral Wire is metal wire sold in short, pre-cut lengths that is painted dark green to help it blend in with herbs and flowers. The wire is sold in several different thicknesses—referred to as gauges—and is used to lengthen stems, reinforce weak stems, and secure bouquets together. Also see spool wire.

Spool Wire is ordinary floral wire sold in one long length on a wooden spool, instead of in shorter, pre-cut lengths. Spool wire is the ideal choice for crafters making wired wreaths or garlands.

Glue Guns are small electrical tools that heat glue to a melting point. The hot glue is expelled when the gun's trigger is manipulated.

Hot Glue is used in a small tool called a glue gun. Sold in small sticks, the glue is inserted into the gun where it is heated to its melting temperature and can then be applied in liquid form. Always use extreme caution when working with hot glue to prevent burns.

Wire Cutters, available in hardware stores, are used for cutting floral wire and will prevent you from yielding to the temptation to use your household or sewing scissors for the task.

illustration A   illustration B   illustration C

One of the most time-saving and enjoyable techniques in herbal crafting is making miniature ("mini") bouquets. If you were making a garland, for instance, using mini bouquets allows you to wire only 30 bouquets (each containing five stems) to the base instead of 150 individual stems. While arranging mini bouquets, many crafters begin to notice marvelous, subtle details in their herbs that they'd previously overlooked.

The number of stems in a mini bouquet is usually determined by the fullness of the materials and the anticipated size of the finished project. Standard mini bouquets are made with 3 to 5 stems, and all materials in each bouquet have the same length. In larger projects, mini bouquets often have as many as 14 stems, and sometimes use stems of varying lengths. A mini bouquet may contain stems of a single type of herb or combine several different herbs together.

After a mini bouquet has been arranged (see illustrations on next page), it is secured together at the stems with a floral pick, floral wire, or floral tape. Extremely delicate materials and stemless blooms can then be hot-glued into the secured mini bouquet if desired.

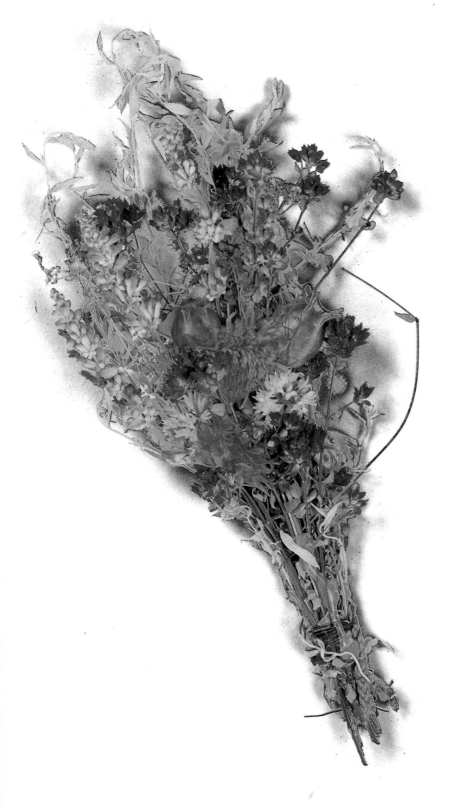

Left: After securing this mini bouquet with floral wire, additional materials, such as the love-in-a-mist seed heads, were hot-glued into the bouquet. Hot glue was also added at the base of the stems for additional security.

Below: Choosing materials whose colors, textures, and shapes contrast, such as the dusty miller and globe amaranth shown here, adds visual interest to mini bouquets.

SECURING A MINI BOUQUET WITH A FLORAL PICK

1a. Position the floral pick against the stems with about an inch (2-1/2 cm.) of overlap. Wrap the wire around the stems several times in the same place, and then spiral the wire down the stems. Trim the stems where the wire ends to make perforation into a foam or straw base easier. Wrap the pick with floral wire. 1b. *Note: mini bouquets secured with floral picks can be wrapped with floral tape, if desired, for additional security.*

SECURING A MINI BOUQUET WITH FLORAL WIRE

2. Lay the stems of the bouquet across a 6-inch (15-cm.) length of wire about an inch from the bottom of the stems. Wrap the wire on the left side around the stems several times in the same place, and spiral the wire on the right down the stems.

SECURING A MINI BOUQUET WITH FLORAL TAPE

3. Position the tape about an inch from the bottom of the stems at a slight angle. Apply enough tension to the tape to make it begin to stretch. Wrap around the stems several times. Cut the tape with scissors.

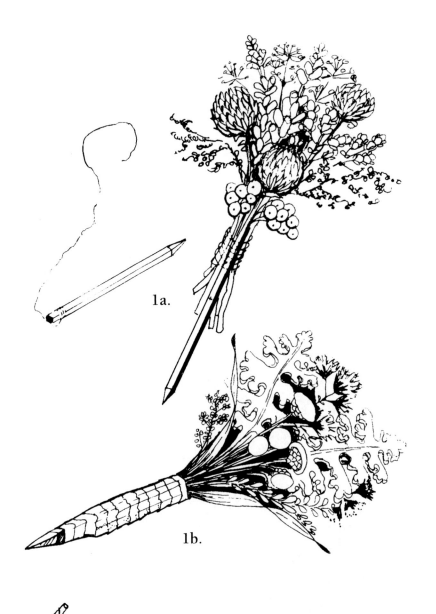

1a.

1b.

3.

2.

With a few exceptions, almost every project in this book is made using a base, and most of these bases are made of floral foam. Floral foam, a dense foam tinted green to help it blend in better with natural materials, is very similar to ordinary Styrofoam. In fact, if you find Styrofoam to be less expensive and more accessible than floral foam in the craft supply stores near your home, then it's perfectly acceptable to use it as a substitute. (Note: Floral foam should not be confused with Oasis foam, which is a very spongelike foam used by florists to extend the life of fresh arrangements.)

Purchase your foam in the largest blocks you can find. As you work on a project you can then cut a piece of foam in the precise size you need and prevent needless waste. The foam cuts easily with an ordinary serrated kitchen knife, and a felt-tip pen can be used to outline the base's shape before cutting, if desired.

A foam base should never show in a finished project. How you disguise the base depends on the type of craft and the way the craft is made. A foam wreath base, for instance, can be covered by wrapping floral tape or ribbon around it. Foam bases for arrangements and topiaries, on the other hand, are generally covered with moss that is secured with floral pins. (A variety of mosses suitable for crafts is available in craft supply stores.) Once a base is covered with tape, ribbon, or moss, your herb materials can be hotglued to it or inserted into it with floral picks or floral wire.

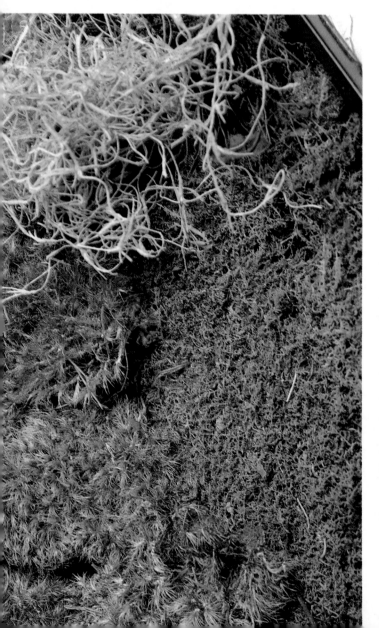

Left: Spanish moss (top) and florist's sheet mosses (below) are popular choices for covering foam bases.

Below: Floral foam and Styrofoam can be cut in creative shapes with an ordinary serrated knife.

HOT GLUE GUNS

Hot glue guns are a lot like microwave ovens—until you use one, you are bound to be skeptical of the ease and speed everyone raves about. Fortunately for crafters, even top-of-the-line glue guns are relatively inexpensive and readily available in hardware and craft stores. If you're a true skeptic, purchase a mini glue gun. Usually available for under five dollars, these glue guns are as effective as their larger counterparts, with the only disadvantage being that you will have to load glue sticks more frequently. Once you've used the mini glue gun with success (or if you've previously used a hot glue gun), you may wish to invest in a low-melt glue gun. New to the craft market, these glue guns use a special glue that melts at a lower temperature, thus eliminating painful burns.

Glue guns are especially valuable when you're working with delicate blooms, when you notice bare spots in a project, when you need to cover the mechanics (such as bare floral wire) of a project, or when you'd like to achieve a more natural-looking angle than you can achieve with floral picks or wire. Perhaps the most wonderful aspect of glue guns, though, is how quickly they let you execute an idea or get carried away in a burst of creativity. The herbal birdhouse on page 118 is a wonderful example of hot glue's potential.

Learning to use a glue gun will take you less than ten minutes. Read the manufacturer's instructions and study the safety tips mentioned below. When you begin working, you may notice strands of dried glue that resemble spider webs. Don't worry about them as you're working; they'll easily pull off later. Avoid being "trigger-happy" with your glue gun — just the smallest dab of hot glue is probably enough to secure an herb in place.

Always keep safety in mind when using a glue gun. Although the melted glue looks harmless, it can burn you severely enough to cause blisters. Keep the following tips in mind: never operate a glue gun when you're tired or distracted; unless your glue gun is cordless, be sure to arrange your work area near an electrical outlet; never leave unsupervised children around a glue

Top: Although slightly more expensive, cordless glue guns allow a crafter unencumbered movement, which helps prevent burns.

gun; find a glass plate or other non-flammable item to rest your glue gun on; always unplug your glue gun as soon as you've finished or if you leave your work area to answer the phone.

OTHER METHODS OF ATTACHMENT

Floral wire and floral clay provide options to the crafter who does not want the attachment to be permanent or cause damage to a special item. Bows are frequently wired so they can be removed and replaced as the designer's whims dictate. In the kitchen arrangement on page 81, the designer used floral clay to hold the two containers together without damaging the antique flour sifter.

Left: Hot glue allows small, delicate herbs, such as rosebuds, to be added to craft projects.

The bows in this book are made from four types of ribbon. Each type offers its own advantages and disadvantages, which you should keep in mind when deciding what type of bow to make.

Traditional cotton and satin ribbons are still favorites with herbal crafters. Although the stiffness of cotton ribbon often makes it difficult to work with, many crafters are unable to resist the incredible variety of patterns and prints offered. Cotton ribbon is also a good choice for beginners; if you're not happy with the finished look of your bow, simply unfold the ribbon, remove any crease marks with a hot iron, and begin again.

Satin ribbon is available in a wide variety of colors and widths, and satin bows impart a loose, whimsical touch to craft projects. Satin ribbon is not a good choice for beginners because it cannot be retied if the bow is tied imperfectly. Satin bows cannot be re-shaped if accidently crushed during shipping or storage, so they should be handled with care.

Two recent ribbon innovations include French ribbon and paper ribbon. French ribbon is generally made from a patterned, translucent fabric that has been lined on the back with several rows of very fine wire. Although it is more expensive than most other types of ribbon, it adds an elegant look to a craft project, is very easy to handle, and can be reshaped easily if crushed.

Sold in a variety of country colors, paper ribbon is easy to work with and can be re-shaped easily. Although it's not as elegant as satin or French ribbon, paper ribbon bows add a fun touch to many country crafts.

HOW TO MAKE A BOW

Step 1. Trim a length of ribbon to 10 inches (25 cm.). Cut each end of the ribbon at an angle. This piece of ribbon will become one of your bow's streamers. Crimp the ribbon in the middle and tightly hold it between your thumb and index finger.

Step 2. Working with a partially un-rolled spool of ribbon, create a second streamer that crosses over the first length of ribbon and crimp it in the middle. Form a 3- to 4-inch (7- to 10-cm.) loop above the crimped point, and a second loop below the crimped point.

Step 3. Make another top and bottom loop the same size as the previous loops. Build the loops side by side instead of on top of each other, and maintain a tight hold on the bow's center. Form two more top and bottom loops that are about 1 inch (2-1/2 cm.) larger than the first loops.

Step 4. Add two more top and bottom loops to the bow that are about 1 inch smaller than the first loops, and position them on top of the large loops. Now create two more top and bottom loops, 3 to 4 inches in length, and position one on either side of the large loops.

Step 5. Form a small finger loop by wrapping the ribbon over the fingers you're using to hold your bow together. Trim the ribbon to match the same angle and length as the first streamer. Insert a precut, 12-inch (30-cm.) length of thin-gauge floral wire through the finger loop and tightly twist both ends of the wire together on the back side of the bow.

Step 6. Shape the bow by rolling your fingers around the inside of each loop, working in the same order as the loops were formed. The bow can now be attached to a craft project with the floral wire or it can be hot-glued in place.

WREATHS

WREATH DESIGN

If you're one of many crafters who feel intimidated by the prospect of "designing" a wreath, keep in mind that a wreath's design often has more to do with the herbs you have available than how creative you are feeling on a particular day. If you have an abundance of a single material and only a few sprigs of colorful blooms, for example, the obvious choice is to design a wreath with a solid background and embellish it with bright accents. The illustrations below explain three basic designs that are simple to create.

METHOD I

Background with Accents. With this design the wreath base is covered with a single background material and accents are then worked into the background. For the best effect, choose accent materials in colors that contrast well with the background. (See examples on pages 42 and 46.)

METHOD II

The Sampler. As their name implies, sampler wreaths are made from a variety of herbs (usually at least five), and the materials tend to be used in more or less equal quantities. Textures and colors are mixed, reflecting the natural variety of the crafter's garden. (See examples on pages 53 and 60.)

METHOD III

Outlining. With this design, the inner and/or outer edges of the wreath are framed with a single material, and the middle surface area is designed separately. With a kitchen wreath, for instance, the inner and outer edges of the base can be covered with bay leaves for an attractive beginning. If you've been staring at a table of herbs and a base for what seems like hours, and inspiration keeps eluding you, this method is a fun way to get started. (See examples on pages 50 and 55.)

ASSEMBLY

While it may look complicated, the actual process of making a wreath is quite simple. Mini bouquets are secured to (or into) a base, and the angle at which the first bouquet is applied is maintained around the base until the surface area is covered. Following is an explanation of each wreathmaking method used in this chapter.

METHOD I

Picking. This method tends to create lush, full wreaths, and is most commonly used with straw bases. (If you're working with a vine base, you may need to add a small amount of hot glue to the tip of each pick before insertion.) The picks are always inserted into the base at an angle, and each new pick covers the wooden portion of the previous pick. The last pick tucks neatly under the first pick to make the start and finish points indistinguishable in the finished wreath.

METHOD II

Wiring. This method tends to create wispier, more delicate looking wreaths. The base is generally made of heavy-gauge wire. A thin-gauge wire is then used to secure small bouquets of herbs

WREATH DESIGN

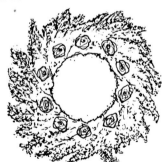

Method I

Method II

Method III

ASSEMBLY

Method I

Method II

to the base. As with a picked wreath, each new bouquet covers the stems of the previous bouquet. A more three-dimensional effect can be created by positioning the bouquets against the wire at different angles.

METHOD III

Hot Gluing. While an important part of wreathmaking, hot-gluing tends to be a supplement to other methods for herbal crafters. If you notice bare spots in a wired thyme wreath, for instance, they can easily be filled in by hot-gluing additional stems of thyme. Hot-gluing is also an ideal way to add small, delicate herbs to a wreath with minimal breakage.

BASES

As wreaths have increased in popularity over the last few years, you've probably noticed many of the beautiful variations in shapes, sizes, and materials being used by contemporary crafters. No matter how creative the contents, however, one constant remains: Every wreath begins with a base. Craft supply stores usually offer a good variety of inexpensive wreath bases in any number of shapes, although if you have access to the materials and/or you plan to produce more than a few wreaths, making your bases at home may become a practical alternative.

MAKING YOUR OWN BASES

WIRE

Materials

Wire cutters, heavy-gauge spool wire or coat hanger

Procedure

1. Cut the wire about 4 inches (10 cm.) longer than needed to form the desired size circular base. *Tip:* Molding the wire around a circular object, such as a large bowl, creates a perfect circle the first time.

2. Allow the circle's ends to overlap for about an inch (2-1/2 cm.), and then secure by wrapping the remaining length around the base.

VINE

Materials

Five to seven fresh-cut vines (grapevines are the most common) cut several inches (5 to 10 cm.) longer than needed to form the desired size base

Procedure

1. Hold four to six vine lengths together and form a circle, allowing an overlap of about 2 inches (5 cm.).

2. Weave the remaining length of vine around the base to secure the vines together.

STRAW

Materials

Several large handfuls of straw, a coat hanger or heavy-gauge wire shaped in a circle, thin-gauge floral wire, wire cutters

Procedure

1. Hold a small handful of straw against the wire circle. Secure it to the wire by tightly wrapping thin-gauge wire around the straw at 2-inch (5-cm.) intervals.

2. Continue repeating step number one until the wire circle is completely covered with straw. Then wrap the wire around three times in the same place and trim it with the wire cutters.

3. Gently mold your straw base into a more perfect circle if necessary.

ASSEMBLY

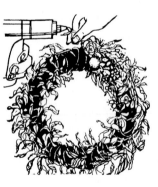

Method III

BASES

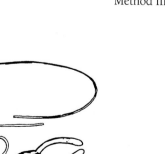

Wire

Vine

Straw

4 0

HERBAL SUNBURST WREATH

Saturated in vibrant color, this wreath combines traditional culinary herbs with a variety of colorful blooms. While the list of plant materials may seem intimidating, remember that you can substitute a smaller base to reduce the number of materials needed.

MATERIALS

14-inch (36-cm.) grapevine
wreath base
Hot glue

15 stems of sweet Annie, trimmed to
10 inches (25 cm.)
10 stems of thyme, trimmed to
3 inches (7 cm.)

70 calendula blossoms
36 Italian oregano blossoms
 8 chive blossoms
32 bee balm blossoms
20 small yarrow heads
28 stems of larkspur, trimmed to
3 inches
24 strawflowers
20 chamomile blossoms

PROCEDURE

1. Weave the stems of sweet Annie into the grapevine base. Hot-glue the stems as needed for reinforcement.
2. Working on the inner edge of the wreath, weave the stems of thyme into the grapevine and hot-glue in place.
3. Using hot glue, cover the remaining surface area of the wreath with blooms, spacing each variety as evenly as possible and positioning them at different angles for a more natural look.

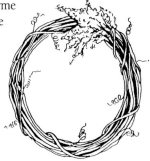

SPICY OREGANO WREATH

The fragrances of Italian oregano,
sweet bay, garlic, sage, star anise, cinnamon,
mountain mint, rosemary, and basil
blend to create the spicy allure
of this kitchen wreath.

MATERIALS

10-inch (25-cm.) straw wreath base
24 floral pins
Hot glue

Approximately 75 stems of fresh-
cut oregano, trimmed to
8 inches (20 cm.)
10 stems each of dried mountain mint,
rosemary, basil, and garden sage,
trimmed to 4 inches (10 cm.)
12 garlic bulbs
4 large heads of yarrow, each divided
into 3 smaller pieces
8 cinnamon sticks cut to 2-inch
(5-cm.) lengths
8 heads of white globe amaranth
8 pieces of star anise
10 stems of dried sweet bay

PROCEDURE

1. Arrange the fresh oregano into 12 mini bouquets (five to six stems per bouquet). Cover the top of the wreath base with oregano bouquets and secure each one to the base with two floral pins.
2. Next cover the inner and outer edges of the base by positioning the oregano bouquets at a slight angle and maintaining that same angle all the way around the base. Hang the oregano wreath in a dry place for seven to ten days.
3. Using hot glue, fill in any bare spots of your wreath with stems of mountain mint, rosemary, cinnamon, basil, and sage.
4. Mentally divide your wreath into four quadrants. In the center of each quadrant, arrange three garlic bulbs and secure them with floral pins. Next, hot-glue three small yarrow blooms and one cinnamon stick around the garlic heads.
5. Accent your wreath with globe amaranth, star anise, bay leaves, and additional cinnamon sticks, using hot glue.

VALENTINE WREATH

Challenged by the myth that most herbs are void
of color, the designer of this wreath arranged
a vibrant burst of herbs on a heart-shaped
base to create a keepsake Valentine gift.

MATERIALS

14-inch (35-cm.) moss heart-
    shaped wreath base
2-1/2 yards (2-1/4 m.) of lace,
    4 inches (10 cm.) wide
Floral pins
Hot glue

16 Queen Anne's lace blooms
45 sprigs of baby's breath, trimmed
    to 3 inches
15 yarrow blooms
30 delphinium blooms
15 sprigs of larkspur, trimmed to
    3 inches
32 strawflowers
32 globe amaranth blooms
15 sprigs of annual statice
 5 sprigs of heather, trimmed to
    4 inches
10 rosebuds

PROCEDURE

1. Place the wreath base face-down on a flat surface and
secure one end of the lace to the bottom point of the heart
with a floral pin. Gather the lace in 1-inch (2-1/2-cm.)
intervals and secure each gather with a floral pin. When
you've returned to the starting point, gather the lace
to overlap the first gather and secure with a floral pin and
trim. Turn the wreath face-up.

2. Position the stems of Queen
Anne's lace, baby's breath,
and yarrow evenly around
the wreath and secure
with hot glue.

3. Repeat the process
with the delphinium,
larkspur, strawflowers,
globe amaranth, statice,
and heather.

4. Fill in any bare spots
with the rosebuds.

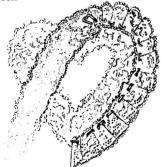

NATURAL HOLIDAY JOY

Crafters are often surprised to discover
that many of the most attractive projects
are made from very simple materials.
The wreath shown here, for example, brings
Christmas cheer and year 'round warmth
with just a few simple garden treasures.

MATERIALS

8-inch (20-cm.) wire ring
Floral tape
1 spool of medium-gauge floral wire
Hot glue

96 stems of sweet Annie, trimmed
to 6 inches (15 cm.)
7 rosebuds
12 stems of pepper berries, trimmed
to 4 inches (10 cm.)
55 ornamental miniature red peppers
4 sprigs of marjoram blooms
8 sprigs of chamomile blooms

PROCEDURE

1. Arrange the sweet Annie into 16 mini bouquets (six stems
per bouquet) and secure each bouquet with floral tape.
2. Hold a single mini bouquet of sweet Annie against the base
at an angle with your left hand and secure by wrapping floral
wire tightly around the stems and base. Position the next
bouquet so it covers the stems of the first bouquet, and again
secure with floral wire. Continue wiring bouquets to the base
until the base is completely covered with sweet Annie.
3. Hot-glue the rosebuds and pepper berries into the middle
area of the wreath.
4. Hot-glue the ornamental
red peppers to the inner and
outer edges of the wreath,
positioning them at interesting angles so they appear to
be growing naturally.
5. As final accents, arrange
sprigs of marjoram and chamomile blooms around the
wreath and hot-glue in place.

SWEET ANNIE WHIMSY

The wire cage base used in this wreath allows designers to easily create a background from scrap pieces of fragrant, delicate sweet Annie. When guests are expected, sweet Annie's fragrance can be rejuvenated by gently rolling a few blooms between your fingers.

MATERIALS

10-inch (25-cm.) wire cage wreath base
Thin-gauge floral wire
Hot glue
Floral tape

2 large handfuls of Sweet Annie
30 4-inch (10-cm.) stems of caspia
6 bee balm blossoms
25 stems of double wild roses, trimmed to 4 inches
Approximately 75 stems of wild grass, trimmed to 4 inches

PROCEDURE

1. Pack the wire cage with small handfuls of sweet Annie and then secure by wrapping with thin-gauge floral wire at 3-inch (7-cm.) intervals.
2. Intermingle stems of caspia into the sweet Annie background by applying a dab of hot glue to single stems of caspia and inserting them at an angle into the sweet Annie.
3. Arrange the wild roses into six mini bouquets (three to five stems per bouquet) and secure each bouquet with floral tape. Next, arrange the wild grass into 25 mini bouquets (three to five stems per bouquet) and secure each bouquet with floral tape.
4. Mentally divide the wreath into six equal sections. Create a bouquet in each section by hot-gluing in bouquets of wild roses, grasses, and a single bee balm blossom.

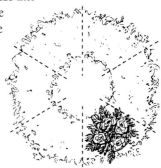

BLOOMING OREGANO WREATH

The lovely design of this wreath is created by decorating the inner circle with dark purple oregano blooms, the middle circle with green wormwood and salad burnet, and the outer circle with delicate ivory feverfew and pearly everlasting.

MATERIALS

10-inch (25-cm.) straw wreath base
75 floral picks
Hot glue

30 stems of oregano, trimmed to
    4 inches (10 cm.)
30 stems of wormwood, trimmed
    to 4 inches
60 stems of salad burnet, trimmed
    to 4 inches
180 stems of pearly everlasting, trimmed
    to 4 inches
60 stems of feverfew, trimmed to
    4 inches
15 stems of globe amaranth
15 stems of pink dianthus

PROCEDURE

1. Prepare the materials by arranging ten mini bouquets of oregano (three stems per bouquet), ten mini bouquets of wormwood (three stems per bouquet), 20 mini bouquets of salad burnet (three stems per bouquet), 20 mini bouquets of pearly everlasting (eight to ten stems per bouquet), and 15 mini bouquets of feverfew (three to five stems per bouquet).

2. Beginning with the inner circle of the wreath base, insert a loose outline of oregano. Fill in any bare areas with feverfew bouquets.

3. Create the middle circle of the wreath by inserting wormwood and salad burnet bouquets. Next, decorate the outer edge of the wreath, first with a row of pearly everlasting and then with a row of feverfew.

4. Using hot glue, add the accent flowers—globe amaranth and pink dianthus— around the wreath.

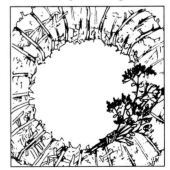

Blue Salvia and Roses Wreath

While many crafters believe a bow distracts from the natural beauty of dried herbs, this blue salvia wreath speaks quite elegantly for itself.

MATERIALS

6-inch (15-cm.) wire ring base
1 spool of floral wire
Hot glue
18 inches (46 cm.) of French ribbon

96 stems of blue salvia, trimmed to 7 inches (17 cm.)
14 miniature roses
6 stems of pepper berries

PROCEDURE

1. Working on a flat surface, separate the salvia into 12 mini bouquets, each one containing eight stems.

2. Hold a single bouquet of salvia against the base at an angle with your left hand and secure by wrapping floral wire tightly around the stems and base. Position the next bouquet so it covers the stems of the first bouquet, and again secure with floral wire. Continue wiring bouquets to the base until the base is completely covered with salvia.

3. Arrange a French ribbon bow around the top of the wreath and hot-glue in place.

4. Space the roses and pepper berries evenly around the wreath, positioning them at various angles and hot-gluing in place.

HISTORICAL HERB MEANINGS

Although many different cultures have ascribed meanings to herbs and flowers over the centuries, the Victorians were the first to combine several meaningful flowers into small bouquets to create messages. Listed below are just a few of the many meaningful herbs.

There is a language, 'little known,'
Lovers claim it as their own.
Its symbols smile upon the land,
Wrought by Nature's wondrous land;
And in their silent beauty speak,
Of life and joy, to those who seek
For Love Divine and sunny hours
In the language of the flowers.
  –The Language of Flowers
      1913

BAY
Glory

BLUE SALVIA
" I think of you"

CHAMOMILE
Energy in Adversity

FENNEL
Worthy of All Praise

GERANIUM
Preference

GLOBE AMARANTH
Unchangeable

LAVENDER
Distrust

MARJORAM
Blushes

MINT
Virtue

NIGELLA
Perplexity

PANSY
Thoughts

SAGE
Esteem

TANSY
" I declare war against you"

SYMBOLIC WEDDING WREATH

Rich in historical meaning as well as beauty, the herbs and flowers in this wedding wreath send a special message to newlyweds. The roses symbolize love; the rosemary stands for remembrance and fidelity; the sage, domestic virtue and wisdom; and the globe amaranth, unfading affection.

(Instructions continue on following page.)

Symbolic Wedding Wreath
(continued from previous page)

MATERIALS

7-inch (17-cm.) straw wreath base
2 feet (61 cm.) white satin ribbon
Floral tape
Hot glue

150 stems of silver king artemisia,
trimmed to 4 inches (10 cm.)
15 stems of sage leaves, trimmed to
4 inches
21 stems of rosemary blooms, trimmed
to 4 inches
20 stems of feverfew, trimmed to
4 inches
40 stems of baby's breath, trimmed to
4 inches
12 rosebuds
12 globe amaranth blooms
3 stems of crested cockscomb
blooms

PROCEDURE

1. Arrange 50 mini bouquets of silver king artemisia (three stems per bouquet), three mini bouquets of sage leaves (five stems per bouquet), three mini bouquets of rosemary blooms (seven stems per bouquet), five mini bouquets of feverfew (four stems per bouquet), and ten mini bouquets of baby's breath (three to five stems per bouquet). Secure each mini bouquet with floral tape.
2. Using hot glue, cover the inner, outer, and top surface areas of the wreath base with bouquets of silver king artemisia.
3. Mentally divide the wreath into three sections and hot-glue one bouquet of sage leaves in the left edge of each. Next, hot-glue a bouquet of rosemary at the base of each bouquet of sage. Follow with four single rosebuds after the rosemary, and four globe amaranth blooms after the roses. Finish each section with a cockscomb bloom.
4. Fill in any bare areas of the wreath with bouquets of feverfew and baby's breath. Tie the ribbon into a bow and hot-glue the bow to the bottom of the wreath. Trim streamers to desired length. (See pages 36 and 37 for complete instructions for making this bow.)

EVERLASTING CENTERPIECE WREATH

Table wreaths made from fresh herbs offer a creative alternative to common vase arrangements. With careful selection of materials, the herbs will dry in place for a permanent centerpiece or wall display.

MATERIALS

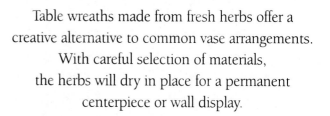

10-inch (25-cm.) straw wreath base
75 wooden floral picks

Approximately 225 stems of the following herbs and flowers, in any combination, trimmed to 4 inches (10 cm.): tansy, silver king artemisia, purple sage, pineapple sage, Mexican sage, Russian sage, Queen Anne's lace, bee balm, cone-flowers, yarrow, feverfew, pennyroyal, catnip, lady's bedstraw, thyme, fennel, chamomile, sundrops, daisies, butterfly bush, peppermint, and spearmint

PROCEDURE

1. Arrange the herbs into 75 mini bouquets (approximately three stems per bouquet) and secure each bouquet with a floral pick.
2. Choosing colors and materials at random, insert the bouquets into the inner and outer edges of the wreath base first. Next, fill in the top surface area with the remaining bouquets.
3. Display the wreath as a table centerpiece while it's still fresh. After the flowers and herbs have dried, fill in any bare spots that may result from shrinkage with additional bouquets of dried herbs and display on a wall.

Fresh Garden Wreath

The delicate color scheme in this wreath is created by arranging the herbs in color groupings— like artists' paints on a palette— and then inserting them into the wreath while still fresh.

MATERIALS

100 floral picks
12-inch (30-cm.) straw wreath base

12 stems of fresh fennel, trimmed to 4 inches (10 cm.)
20 stems each of the following fresh materials, trimmed to 4 inches: calendula, lemon balm, lavender, fennel, sweet bay, lemon verbena, sage, scented geraniums, oregano, yarrow, lovage, chives, bee balm, peppermint, and goldenrod

PROCEDURE

1. Arrange the fennel into four mini bouquets (three stems per bouquet) and secure each bouquet with a floral pick. Set aside.

2. Arrange the remaining materials into 96 mini bouquets (three stems per bouquet) that each contain materials of similar color.

3. Working with all of the materials except the fennel, begin inserting bouquets into the inner edge of the wreath base. When the inner edge is covered, begin working on the outer edge.

4. Now fill in the top surface of the wreath with mini bouquets. Mentally divide the wreath into four quadrants and insert a bouquet of fennel in the center of each one.

5. After the herbs have dried (approximately two weeks), fill in any bare areas that result from shrinkage with additional bouquets of dried herbs.

Spring
Garden Wreath

One of the most enjoyable aspects of wreathmaking is choosing from the many possible design styles and variations. On the wreath shown here, for instance, the top half of the vine base has been left bare to create an outdoor planter effect. The wreath displays as well on shelves as it does on walls.

MATERIALS

10-inch (25-cm.) grapevine
    wreath base
Craft glue
Thin-gauge floral wire
Floral tape
Pencil

1 small handful each of sphagnum
    moss and ground pine
10 fern fronds
    Approximately 10 stems each of
    dried oregano, bee balm, lark-
    spur, wild grass, and wild rose

PROCEDURE

1. Glue the sphagnum moss to the inside bottom of the wreath, allowing it to extend over the edges. Using the pointed end of a pencil, create small holes in the sphagnum moss. Place a small dab of craft glue in each hole and insert a sprig of ground pine.

2. Wire and wrap all plant materials. Trim the wire stems to 4 inches (10 cm.). Beginning with the fern, create an outline for the arrangement by inserting the wired stems through the moss and into the vines of the base. (Dab each stem with craft glue before inserting.) Fill out the arrangement with stems of oregano, bee balm, larkspur, wild grasses, and wild roses.

3. After the glue has dried, trim away any wired stems that extend below the wreath base.

AUTUMN CELEBRATION WREATH

An interesting variety of seed heads and blooms
in neutral shades of brown and cream are used
to create the background for this wreath.
Strawflowers, statice, and safflowers
add vibrant bursts of color.

MATERIALS

10-inch (25-cm.) straw wreath base
50 floral picks
8-inch (20-cm.) twig
Hot glue
Small artificial bird

Approximately 200 stems of the
following herbs and flowers, in
any combination, trimmed to
3 inches (7 cm.): astilbe,
chamomile, silver germander,
Queen Anne's lace, lamb's ear,
feverfew, wormwood, and
yarrow
12 strawflowers
20 stems of purple statice, trimmed
to 3 inches
10 safflower blooms
5 sweet-gum balls

PROCEDURE

1. Arrange 50 mini bouquets (three to five stems per
bouquet) of astilbe, chamomile, silver germander, Queen
Anne's lace, lamb's ear, feverfew, wormwood, and yarrow.
Each bouquet should contain herbs of varying texture,
size, and color.
2. Secure each mini bouquet to a floral pick. Insert the
bunches into the base to create a background, leaving small
bare spots.
3. Using hot glue, fill in the bare spots with strawflowers,
purple statice, safflowers,
and sweet-gum balls.
4. Attach the twig or branch
to the wreath with small
dabs of hot glue and hot-
glue the bird to the branch.
5. To create a more natural
look, hot-glue small stems
of statice under the bird
and around the twig.

Wispy Blue Salvia Wreaths

Small herb wreaths displayed in pairs
create a charming, inviting atmosphere
in any room. The wreaths here are both made
with backgrounds of blue salvia and caspia,
although they are each accented with different
selections of herbs, flowers, and ribbon.

MATERIALS

For both wreaths:

6-inch (15-cm.) metal ring base
1 spool of medium-gauge floral wire
1 spool of thin-gauge floral wire
Green floral tape
Craft glue
180 stems of salvia, trimmed to
6 inches (15 cm.) for each wreath
25 stems of caspia, trimmed to
3 inches (7 cm.) for each wreath

Accent materials for the wreath shown left:

10 wild roses
5 to 8 blue pansies
4-1/2 feet (138 cm.) of 1/8-inch
(1/3-cm.) double-faced navy
blue satin ribbon

Accent materials for the wreath shown right:
  10 wild roses
    4-1/2 feet (138 cm.) of 1/8-inch
    (1/3-cm.) double-faced pink
    satin ribbon

PROCEDURE

1. Prepare the salvia by arranging it in 30 mini bouquets (five or six stems per bouquet). Because the salvia is so delicate, do not secure the bouquets with tape, wire, or picks.

2. Hold one bouquet of salvia by the stems against the wire base and secure by wrapping with spool wire. (See page 39 for complete directions for this type of wreathmaking.) Continue securing salvia bouquets to the ring base until it's completely covered. Some breakage is to be expected, so save broken salvia stems and glue them into any bare spots you may notice in the wreath.

3. Wire and wrap the caspia and accent flowers with thin-gauge wire. Working with one stem at a time, place a small dab of craft glue onto the end of the wire and insert it deeply enough in the salvia so that only the flower head shows. Be sure to insert the flowers at the same angle as the salvia.

4. Cut the satin ribbon into three 18-inch (46-cm.) lengths. Holding the three ribbon lengths together, twist a 4-inch (10-cm.) length of thin-gauge floral wire around the middle. Dab the wire with glue and insert into the salvia.

Naturally Simple Heart Wreaths

Herbs such as tarragon and thyme
are often overlooked by herbal crafters
in favor of more vibrantly colored materials.
These two heart wreaths reveal the natural
beauty of such simple garden herbs.

MATERIALS

For Tarragon and Silver Santolina Wreath, left:

Wire coat hanger or heavy gauge
wire
Green floral tape
Hot glue
Medium-sized cotton or satin bow

Approximately 30 stems of fresh
silver santolina, trimmed to
4 inches (10 cm.)
Approximately 40 stems of fresh
tarragon, trimmed to 4 inches

MATERIALS

For Thyme Wreath, above:

5-inch (12-cm.) heart-shaped
foam wreath base
Green floral tape
1 floral pin
Hot glue
Small cotton bow

Approximately 200 stems
of thyme, trimmed to
1-1/2 inches (4 cm.)

PROCEDURE

1. Bend the coat hanger or wire into a heart shape, overlap and secure the ends, and wrap the entire base with floral tape.
2. Arrange seven mini bouquets of silver santolina and ten mini bouquets of tarragon (three to five stems per bouquet). Secure together by wrapping with floral tape.
3. Starting at the bottom of the heart, hot-glue a single mini bouquet of santolina to the right side of the base. Next, position a single bouquet of tarragon so that it overlaps the stems of the santolina and hot-glue in place. Continue attaching the bouquets in this same way, alternating santolina and tarragon until you reach the top center of the heart.
4. Again starting at the bottom of the heart, hot-glue bouquets to the left side of the base, using the same techniques described above.
5. Experiment with locations for the bow and then hot-glue in place.

PROCEDURE

1. Prepare the foam wreath base by wrapping it with floral tape. Bend a floral pin in half and insert into the back of the base to create a hanger.
2. Arrange the thyme into approximately 50 mini bouquets (three to five stems per bouquet) and secure each bouquet by wrapping floral tape around the stems.
3. Lay a mini bouquet against the wreath base and secure with hot glue. Continue hot-gluing mini bouquets until the entire wreath base is covered, taking care to always hot-glue the bouquets at the same angle.
4. Fill in any bare spots on the wreath by hot-gluing in single stems of thyme and finish by hot-gluing a small bow to the wreath.

Blooming
Pastel Wreath

The fascinating variety of herb and flower blooms in this pastel wreath is a wonderful remembrance of the summer splendors of your garden during the winter months. All of the materials in this wreath are air dried by simply hanging them upside down in a dark, dry room for several weeks.

MATERIALS

10-inch (25-cm.) straw wreath base
55 wooden floral picks
Hot glue

60 stems of double wild roses, trimmed to 4 inches (10 cm.)
10 stems of wild yarrow, trimmed to 4 inches
90 stems of oregano blooms, trimmed to 4 inches
15 Korean mint blooms
15 bee balm blooms

PROCEDURE

1. Arrange the double wild roses into 20 mini bouquets (three stems per bouquet), the wild yarrow into 5 mini bouquets (two stems per bouquet), and the oregano into 30 mini bouquets (three stems per bouquet). Secure together with wooden floral picks.

2. Beginning with the inner circle, insert two rows of double wild roses.

3. Cover the remaining surface area of the wreath with wild yarrow, oregano blooms, and additional double wild roses.

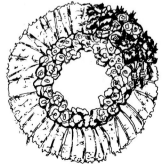

4. Using hot glue, fill in bare spots with Korean mint and bee balm blooms.

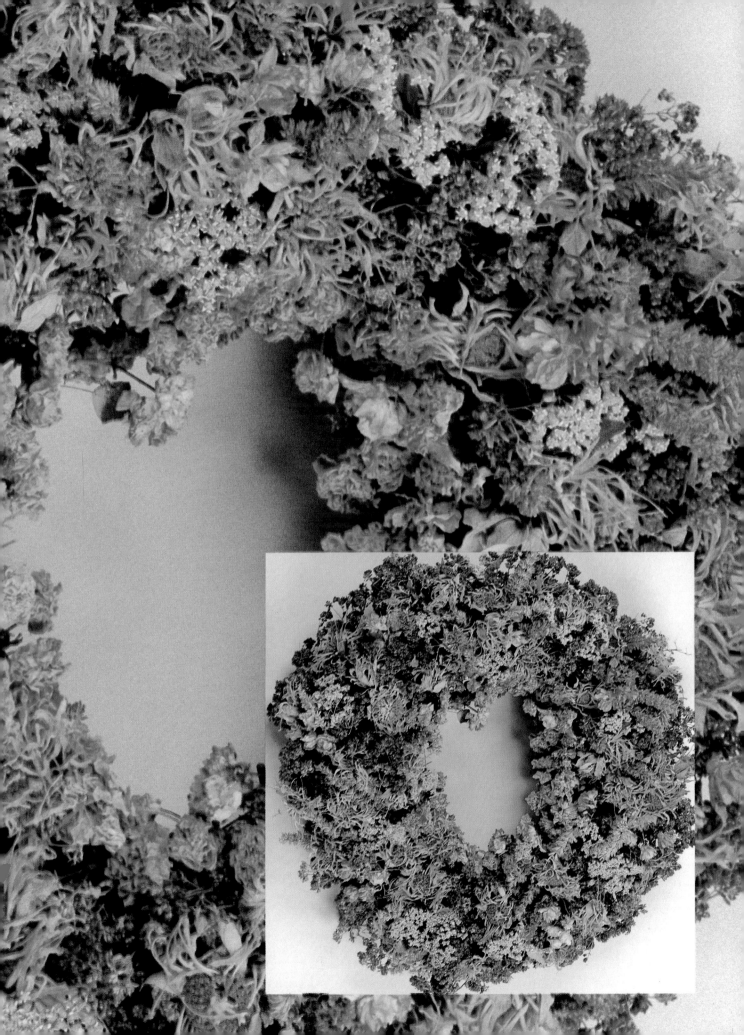

TOPIARIES

The unusual shapes of craft topiaries often produce extreme reactions: people either find them lovely and elegant or out and out unattractive. Historically, living topiaries were a revered art form. They were used to decorate gardens and worn as elaborate headdresses. During a masked ball in 1745, Louis XV disguised himself as a yew tree topiary to win the heart of a young lady who loved gardening.

Herbal craft topiaries are made by constructing a topiary form and then decorating it. Topiary forms are available pre-assembled at many craft supply stores, but they are relatively simple to make and you probably already have most of the materials.

The topiary form consists of three parts: the container (usually a clay flower pot), the stem, and the foam form. The topiary's stem is first secured in the container. This can be accomplished by positioning the stem in the middle of the container and pouring plaster of Paris around it, or by cutting a piece of floral foam to fit inside the container and then inserting the stem securely into the foam. (With the latter method you may need to weight the bottom of the container to prevent a larger topiary from tipping over.)

To complete the topiary form, insert the top end of the stem about three-fourths of the way into the foam form. Remove the stem, fill most of the hole in the form with hot glue, and then re-insert the stick. Then cover the foam base with moss, if desired, and decorate with dried herbs.

The last, and perhaps most important, step to completing a topiary is covering the plaster of Paris or foam in the container and adding small accents around the bottom of the stem that give the topiary a more natural-looking appearance. These accents often include dried mushrooms, tree fungus, moss, lichen, and even small sprigs of herb blooms.

SPRING TOPIARY

Decorative spring topiaries are portable enough to move from room to room and their delicate fragrances gently scent the air around them. The topiary shown here combines herbs, flowers, and ground pine for a fresh-from-the-garden look.

MATERIALS

Craft glue
Green floral tape
1 box of toothpicks
Hot glue
Thin-gauge floral wire
1 small clay flowerpot
4-inch (10-cm.) foam ball
2 fishing weights
1 length of 1/2-inch (1-1/4-cm.) wooden dowel cut to 12 inches (30 cm.) and stained to the color of your choice
1 small block of floral foam

Sheet moss
Approximately 10 stems each of dried oregano, wild roses, dianthus, German statice, miniature roses, globe amaranth, verbena, blue salvia, cornflowers, feverfew, marguerite, wild yarrow, mountain knapweed, annual statice, bee balm, and chamomile
Ground pine

PROCEDURE

1. Hot-glue two fishing weights to the bottom center inside the clay pot.
2. Prepare the topiary's base, stem, and form as described on page 69. Note: The dowel serves as the stem.
3. Working in small sections at a time, cover the foam ball and the foam in the clay pot with sheet moss using hot glue.
4. Using the dried herbs and flowers, create 53 mini bouquets of three stems each. (You will need approximately 40 bouquets to cover the ball and 10 to cover the foam at the topiary's base.) Wire and wrap each bouquet and trim the stems to approximately 1/2 inch. Working with one bouquet at a time, dab a small amount of craft glue on the end of each stem and insert it into the ball. Leave small spaces around the bouquets for the ground pine.
5. Using an awl or other sharp object, make small holes around the bouquets and insert pieces of ground pine. Repeat steps 4 and 5 to decorate the topiary's base.

YARROW AND ROSES TOPIARY

The lush beauty of this tall topiary is achieved with a generous use of yarrow and pink roses. The topiary can be dressed up with a lace doily and displayed indoors, or placed in a winter garden and allowed to fade gently with time.

(Instructions on following page)

MATERIALS

4-inch (10-cm.) clay pot
Plaster of Paris
5-inch (12-cm.) foam ball
12-inch (30-cm.) -long branch,
    1 inch (2-1/2 cm.) in
    diameter
Hot glue
Small ribbon bow

Sheet moss
35 large heads of yarrow, each
    separated into 3 smaller heads
10 sweetheart roses
10 miniature roses

PROCEDURE

1. Prepare the topiary's base, stem, and form as described on page 69.
2. Working in small sections at a time, cover the ball with sheet moss using hot glue.
3. Decorate the ball with yarrow by making 1/4-inch (.60-cm.) holes in the ball with a pencil, dabbing each yarrow stem with hot glue, and inserting into a hole.
4. Position both varieties of roses around the topiary to fill in any bare spots and secure with hot glue.
5. Decorate the base of the topiary by hot-gluing sheet moss to the plaster and gluing a small bow to the pot.

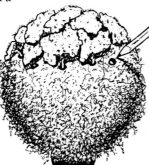

TRIANGLE TOPIARY

Topiaries needn't be round or conical.
Here's one in a different, yet
eye-pleasing, triangular shape.

MATERIALS

For topiary on page 74:

    Clay pot
    Handful of pepples
    Potting mix
    Raffia or plastic twist ties
    Heavy wire (like a coat hanger)
        about three times as long as
        you want your topiary to be high

    Rooted cuttings or small plants of
        rosemary, myrtle, lemon
        verbena, santolina, sweet bay
        or ivy

PROCEDURE

1. Bend the heavy wire into a triangle shape, with the cut ends twisted together in the center of the bottom to form a 3- to 4-inch stake to stick into the soil.
2. Select two plants, or one plant with two branches growing in a wide V. Ivy is by far the easiest plant to use for this type of topiary. Put a few pebbles in the clay pot, fill it partway with potting mix, settle the plants close together in the center with their shoots pointing sideways and in opposite directions, and firm the mix around their roots. Insert the wire form into the soil.
3. Gently bend and wrap the plant shoots around the wire form, one on each side, and tie with bits of raffia where necessary. Ivy won't need much trimming. For other plants, pinch out side shoots as they form to encourage upward growth. As the plants grow, continue winding them gently around the wire. Let ivy grow up one side, and down the opposite side, and back around again, tucking the new growth in among the older leaves until the form is well covered and full. Other plants can be trained back down the opposite side when they reach the peak, or the tips can be pinched out when they meet.
4. Follow the instructions in steps 4, 5, and 6 of the double-ball procedure for watering, re-potting, and pruning techniques.

time. Continue to remove side shoots again until the main shoot reaches the height of the upper ball. Then allow side shoots to remain for the upper ball. When the main shoot reaches an inch or so short of the final height, pinch out the tip. When this vertical tip is removed, the plant will redirect its growth energy into the side branches. When these side branches each have two or three sets of leaves, pinch out their tips so that more branches will form. Continue pinching out tips until you're happy with the size and fullness of the topiary.

4. Water your growing topiary when the soil appears dry. Fertilize monthly with a diluted solution of fish emulsion February through September and withhold feedings October through January. To ensure compact growth, the topiary will need good light from a sunny window. Turn the pot every few days so the topiary will grow evenly.

5. Make it a routine to check the raffia ties every two weeks to make sure they're not cutting into the stem because of growth. Loosen the ties if necessary. Also check to see if it's time for repotting. If you are watering daily and the soil still seems dry, the pot has probably filled with roots and there's little or no soil left to retain moisture. Carefully repot in a large pot.

6. Once your topiary has reached a height and shape you like, you still need to prune it occasionally. Always work at eye level with the topiary, and position the tip of your pruning shears in the direction you want the leaves to grow. Use tweezers to remove any dead interior leaves. Once the stem becomes woody, you may be able to remove the stake.

DOUBLE BALL TOPIARY

Living topiaries have been delighting herbal gardeners for centuries, and their designs are limited only by your imagination.

MATERIALS

For topiary on page 75:
Clay pot
Handful of pebbles
Potting mix
Raffia or plastic twist ties
1 slender, sturdy stake about 6 inches taller than your finished topiary will be

1 rooted cutting or small plant of rosemary, myrtle, lemon verbena, santolina, or sweet bay

PROCEDURE

1. Choose a plant with a strong, straight stem and an unpinched growing tip. Put a few pebbles in the clay pot, fill it partway with potting mix, settle the plant in the center with the shoot pointing straight up, and firm the mix around the roots.

2. Place the stake parallel to the plant's stem and insert it into the pot until you feel it hit the bottom. Secure the stake to the stem at intervals of about 2 inches (5 cm.) with raffia. Position the raffia's knots so they rest against the stake, and make sure the raffia is loose enough to prevent damaging the delicate stem.

3. To encourage growth in height, carefully remove any side shoots that are growing along the topiary's stem from about an inch below the tip. Allow leaves to remain for photosynthesis. Mark the stake where you want the finished balls to be. Allow side shoots to remain on the section of stem that will be the lower ball. Pinch out the tips of these side shoots when they have two or three sets of leaves, but don't tip out the main shoot by mistake at the same

MINIATURE TOPIARIES

Made with small herb blooms, these miniature topiaries are a wonderful way to display smaller, often unnoticed treasures from your garden.

MATERIALS

For Potpourri Topiary, below left:
Small planter
2-inch (5-cm.) foam ball
Small block of floral foam
4-inch (10-cm.) -long branch,
1/4-inch (.60 cm.) in diameter
3 12-inch (30-cm.) lengths of
narrow yellow satin ribbon
Hot glue
Small feather

1/4 cup (.06 liter) of potpourri
made from dried strawflowers,

marigolds, yarrow, tansy
blooms, coneflowers, and
chamomile
Small handful of sheet moss
Small cluster of tree fungus
Note: For potpourri instructions, see pages 136–137.

PROCEDURE

1. Prepare the topiary's base, stem, and form as described on page 69.
2. Working in small sections at a time, cover the foam ball with hot glue and roll in potpourri.
3. Hold all three ribbon lengths together and tie them into a simple bow. Hot-glue the bow to the top of the ball and arrange the streamers in even intervals.
4. Hot-glue small pieces of moss to the foam base of the topiary. Insert the feather into the moss and hot-glue the tree fungus around the stem.

MATERIALS

For Rose Petal Topiary, below center:

Small planter
Small block of floral foam
4-inch (10-cm.) -long branch,
    1/4-inch (.60 cm.) in diameter
4-inch-tall foam cone
Small plaid bow
Hot glue

Small handful of sheet moss
Small cluster of lichen
Approximately 25 dried rose petals
20 peppermint leaves, dried and
    crushed

PROCEDURE

1. Prepare the topiary's base, stem, and form as described on page 69.
2. Working in small sections at a time, cover the foam cone with crushed peppermint leaves using hot glue.
3. Starting at the top of the cone, begin hot-gluing rose petals to the cone, working them down and around until the cone is covered.
4. Hot-glue small pieces of moss to the foam base of the topiary. Hot-glue the bow and the lichen to the moss.

MATERIALS

For Rosebud Topiary, below right:

Small planter
Small block of floral foam
4-inch (10-cm.) -long branch,
    1/4-inch (.60 cm.) in diameter
2-inch (5-cm.) foam ball
3 12-inch (30-cm.) lengths of
    narrow satin ribbon in
    assorted colors
Hot glue

20 peppermint leaves, dried and
    crushed
Approximately 25 miniature
    rosebuds
Small handful of sheet moss
Decorative tree fungus

PROCEDURE

1. Prepare the topiary's base, stem, and form as described on page 69.
2. Working in small sections at a time, cover the foam ball with crushed peppermint leaves using hot glue.
3. Starting at the top of the ball, begin hot-gluing rosebuds to the ball, working them down and around until the ball is covered.
4. Hold all three ribbon lengths together and tie them into a simple bow. Hot-glue the bow to the base and trim the streamers if desired.
5. Hot-glue small pieces of moss to the foam base of the topiary. As a final touch, hot-glue a small piece of tree fungus into the moss, positioning it to appear growing naturally.

ARRANGEMENTS AND BOUQUETS

CHOOSING A CONTAINER

Choosing containers for herbal arrangements can be as much fun as actually making the arrangements. A discerning eye cast around your home or local antique shops usually provides exciting prospects. Some interesting containers to look for include country baskets, glass serving bowls, antique hat boxes, tea pots and accessories, flour sifters, and so on. Any freestanding vessel will work, and the more creative you are with a container, the more enjoyment you'll have from displaying your final arrangement.

PREPARING YOUR CONTAINER

With few exceptions, almost every container will need to be prepared with floral foam before it's ready for arranging. The foam can be purchased in craft supply stores in a wide range of sizes and shapes. Often, the most economical choice is to buy a large block of foam that can be divided up and used for several projects.

The foam will first need to be cut to fit the inside of your container. An ordinary kitchen knife with a serrated blade works well. Many crafters find it helpful to trace the shape of the bottom of the container onto the foam instead of guessing. However you choose to work, the ultimate goal is a piece of foam that fits snugly into the container and does not protrude over the top. To increase the ultimate stability of the arrangement you may wish to glue small fishing weights to the bottom of the foam before securing it in your container.

Next, the foam will need to be secured in the container with tape, wire, or hot glue. Your choice of adhesive should be based on convenience and the value of the container. With an inexpensive basket, for example, hot glue would work fine; if the basket were an antique Shaker collectible, wire or tape would work just as well without damaging the basket. Finally, use floral pins to cover all visible areas of foam with moss.

CREATING THE ARRANGEMENT

Although professional designers and home crafters often create their arrangements with identical materials, the finished products often look very different, much to the frustration of crafters. The crucial, invisible difference is the awareness of shape and depth that professionals have.

The shape of your arrangement— whether it be oval, round, or triangular— should first be considered when you choose your container. A low, oval-shaped bowl (see the arrangement on page 86), for instance, would be well complemented by an oval-shaped arrangement.

As you begin to insert stems of herbs into your foam base, envision the shape you'd like to create. Working with one or two herbs of similar color, establish the perimeters of your arrangement. (See illustration.) Now choose a specific herb to serve as your arrangement's focal point and insert several stems of this herb around the arrangement, echoing the shape of the perimeter. Last, fill in your arrangement with remaining herbs.

The second important element of good design is depth. The focal herbs, for example, should protrude outward slightly more than the background herbs, and the filler herbs should be positioned at a variety of depths. Placing darker-colored herbs near the center of an arrangement tends to draw the eye inward and creates the illusion of depth.

Country Kitchen Arrangement

Using two unusual containers, as shown on page 81—a collectible cracker tin on the left and an antique flour sifter on the right—helps create the strong visual appeal of this arrangement.

MATERIALS

Cracker tin
Flour sifter
Floral foam
Floral clay
Medium-gauge floral wire
2 wooden spoons

30 rose hips
30 sprigs of sage
3 dried pomegranates
6 stems of boneset, trimmed to
   10 inches (25 cm.)
15 stems of coneflowers, trimmed
   to 10 inches
45 stems of globe amaranth, trimmed
   to 8 inches (20 cm.)

PROCEDURE

1. Secure the two containers together with floral clay. Prepare the arrangement's base by cutting pieces of floral foam to fit inside each container.
2. Prepare the herbal materials by lengthening the stems of rose hips, sage, and pomegranates with floral wire to eight inches. Cut the stems of the boneset, coneflowers, and globe amaranth at a sharp angle.
3. Create the outline of the arrangement with the sage. Next, space the boneset, coneflowers, rose hips, and globe amaranth around the arrangement.
4. Insert the two wooden spoons into the foam in the back of the arrangement.
5. Last, insert the pomegranates into the arrangement, allowing the dried materials to cushion them.

Fireplace Basket Arrangement

The fireplaces that add such warmth and charm to our homes during the winter often become eyesores during spring and summer months. The solution? A colorful hearth basket filled with the vibrant beauty of blooming herb gardens.

MATERIALS

Large basket to fit your fireplace
   (18 × 20 inches, 46 × 50 cm.
   shown here)
Floral foam
Medium-gauge floral wire
Hot glue
Sheet moss
French ribbon tied in a bow
   with 5-inch (12-cm.) streamers

50 stems of sweet Annie, trimmed
   to 18 inches
8 chive blossoms, trimmed to
   18 inches
12 chive seed heads, trimmed
   to 18 inches
12 sprigs of Mexican sage
36 zinnia blooms (dried in silica gel)
1 large bunch of tansy blossoms
1 pansy (dried in silica gel)

PROCEDURE

1. Prepare the arrangement's base by cutting a piece of foam to fit the inside of the basket and secure with hot glue.
2. Create a two-inch green border near the top of the basket by hot-gluing sheet moss around the basket.
3. Position the bow and its streamers under the green border and hot-glue in place.
4. Prepare the herbal materials by cutting the stems of sweet Annie at a sharp angle. Lengthen the stems of the chive blossoms and seed heads, the sage, and the zinnias to 18 inches with floral wire.
5. Create the arrangement's outline by inserting the sweet Annie directly into the foam base in small bunches. Position two-thirds of the stems in front of the handle and the remaining one-third behind the handle.
6. Fill in the remaining spaces in front of the handle with the chive and sage stems and 30 zinnia stems. Position the remaining six zinnia stems behind the handle.
7. Embellish the green border by hot-gluing tansy blossoms and a single pansy into the moss.

Keepsake Bridal Bouquet

This large herbal bouquet was created as a special gift for the bride with herbs dried from her bridal bouquet. The bouquet can be displayed flat on a table or hung on a wall.

MATERIALS

Thin-gauge floral wire
Green floral tape
25-inch (63 cm.) length of
    satin ribbon

6 stems of sweet Annie, trimmed
    to 14 inches (36 cm.)
6 stems of achillea 'The Pearl',
    trimmed to 14 inches
9 stems of blue salvia, trimmed
    to 12 inches (30 cm.)
7 stems of chive blooms
9 stems of yarrow
7 stems of goldenrod
5 pink roses

PROCEDURE

1. Working on a flat surface, create a fan-shaped arrangement with the sweet Annie and achillea 'The Pearl'. Create a second layer to the arrangement with the blue salvia.

2. Prepare the remaining materials by lengthening eight stems to 10 inches (25 cm.), five stems to 9 inches (22 cm.), five stems to 8 inches (20 cm.), five stems to 7 inches (17 cm.), and five stems to 6 inches (15 cm.).

3. Continue adding new layers to the bouquet, starting with the longest stems and working down to the shortest.

4. Cut a length of floral wire to 12 inches and wrap it with floral tape. Hold the bouquet just above the last row of herbs and wrap the wire around it at least four times. Twist the wire's ends together in the back and pull tight. Form a loop in the wire for hanging, if desired.

5. Tie a large bow around the wire with the satin ribbon.

WICKER BASKET ARRANGEMENT

The fluffy texture of achillea 'The Pearl' blooms provides an enchanting background for the herbal materials in this arrangement. The wicker basket creates a casual, country look that can easily be dressed up with a lace doily.

MATERIALS

Floral foam
Medium-gauge wire
Green floral tape
Adhesive floral tape
Floral pins
Sphagnum moss
Wicker basket

15 stems of sweet Annie
26 stems of white yarrow
55 stems of achillea 'The Pearl'
6 pink roses
19 stems of pink dianthus
18 stems of blue salvia

PROCEDURE

1. Prepare the arrangement's base by cutting a block of foam to fit inside the basket. Trim the foam flush with the top of the basket and secure with adhesive floral tape. Cover the foam with moss, using floral pins as needed to hold the moss in place.
2. Using medium-gauge wire, lengthen the stems of sweet Annie, white yarrow, and achillea 'The Pearl' to 15 inches (39 cm.) Lengthen all other stems to 13 inches (33 cm.).
3. Create the oval shape of the arrangement with sweet Annie. Complete the background with white yarrow and achillea 'The Pearl'.
4. Fill out the arrangement with remaining materials, saving the blue salvia for last to prevent damaging them.

Bridal Hat Bouquet

Herbs and flowers have been a welcome part of weddings for centuries. And while large bouquets are probably the most popular choices, smaller bouquets often add a special touch.

MATERIALS

1 roll each of heavy-duty dark green and beige thread
Embroidery needle
18-inch (46-cm.) length of 2-inch (5-cm.)-wide ivory satin ribbon

8 stems of chamomile blooms
5 stems of anise hyssop
5 stems of mealy cup sage
2 stems of achillea 'The Pearl'
3 stems of Mexican sage blossoms
3 'Simplicity' roses
2 stems of chive blossoms
2 stems of marguerite
1 stem of calendula

Note: All materials should be trimmed to 4 inches (10 cm.) in length

PROCEDURE

1. Arrange the chamomile and anise hyssop in a fan shape. Next, add the mealy cup sage, achillea 'The Pearl', Mexican sage, roses, chives, and marguerite to the bouquet. Finish with a single stem of calendula in the center.

2. Secure the bouquet by tying green thread around the stems. Trim the stems even.

3. Thread an embroidery needle with beige thread and gently baste the bouquet to the hat. Do not cut the thread.

4. Tie the ribbon into a bow. Position it against the bouquet and baste in place. Then knot the thread, and clip the ends. Trim the bow's streamers to the desired length.

ANTIQUE BOWL ARRANGEMENT

With over 150 stems of herbs, this large table arrangement uses a variety of garden favorites to create a show-stopping centerpiece. To prevent fading, remember not to display the arrangement in a location receiving direct sunlight.

MATERIALS

Medium-gauge floral wire
Green floral tape
Floral foam
Adhesive floral tape
Floral pins
Sphagnum moss
Antique bowl

26 stems of sweet Annie
16 stems of white yarrow
10 stems of achillea 'The Pearl'
18 stems of coneflowers
30 stems of caspia
6 stems of Mexican sage
12 stems of larkspur
6 stems of pink chive blossoms
7 stems of lavender
8 stems of catnip
6 pink roses
9 stems of cockscomb
10 stems of blue salvia

PROCEDURE

1. Prepare the arrangement's base by cutting a block of foam to fit inside the bowl. Trim the foam flush with the top of the bowl and secure with adhesive floral tape. Cover the foam with moss, using floral pins as needed to hold the moss in place.

2. Using medium-gauge floral wire, lengthen the stems of sweet Annie, white yarrow, and achillea 'The Pearl' to 15 inches (39 cm.). Lengthen all other stems to 13 inches (33 cm.).

3. Create the oval shape of the arrangement with an outline of sweet Annie. Complete the background with white yarrow and achillea 'The Pearl'.

4. Fill out the arrangement with remaining materials.

TEA TABLE ARRANGEMENTS

For those of us who can't resist collecting special teacups and saucers, these small arrangements add herbal charm and beauty when displayed with a collection. The arrangement on the left uses a polished door knob as its container, while the arrangement on the right is in a small creamer.

MATERIALS

For Roses and Statice, below left:

    Aluminum door knob
    Handful of sand
    Small scrap of floral foam
    Serrated knife
    Hot glue

    Approximately 15 stems of German statice, trimmed to 3-inch (7-1/2 cm.) lengths
    10 stems of 'Sweetheart' roses, trimmed to 2-inch (5-cm.) lengths

PROCEDURE

1. Prepare the container by polishing the door knob and filling it with sand. Cut a scrap piece of foam to fit the diameter of the door knob, about 1/2-inch (1-1/4 cm.) deep. Wedge the foam inside the neck of the door knob.

2. Create a low, round shape to the arrangement with the German statice by inserting the stems at different depths in the foam.

3. Apply a small dab of hot glue to each rose stem and position it in the statice.

foam insert

MATERIALS

For Creamer arrangement, below right:

    Small creamer
    Floral foam
    Serrated knife
    Florist's sheet moss
   3 floral pins
    Hot glue

40 stems, in any combination, trimmed to 2 to 3 inches (7 to 10 cm.) of the following herbs and flowers: scented geranium foliage, 'Sweetheart' rose blooms, wild yarrow blooms, chrysanthemum blooms, love-in-a-mist seed heads, heather, black-eyed Susan blooms, silver santolina foliage, feverfew blooms, Queen Anne's lace blooms, German statice blooms, tarragon foliage, and sterlingia foliage

PROCEDURE

1. Prepare the base by cutting a piece of floral foam to fit inside the creamer. Insert the foam into the creamer and cover the top of the foam with moss. Secure the moss to the foam with floral pins.

2. Examine the stems of your materials and separate them in two piles: one pile with stems strong enough to insert directly into the foam; and the other pile with delicate, weak stems. Cut the ends of all the sturdy stems at a sharp angle.

3. Create a low, round shape to the arrangement by inserting the materials with sturdy stems at different depths in the foam.

4. Fill out the arrangement by hot-gluing the delicate stems against the sturdier stems.

Herbal Winter Wonderland

Silvery lamb's ear and fragrant evergreens
are used to create the arrangement shown
on page 93. As Christmas approaches,
red glass tree ornaments and other holiday
knickknacks can easily be attached to
floral picks and added to the arrangement.

MATERIALS

Low basket
5-inch (12-cm.) foam ball
Serrated knife
14-inch (36-cm.) length of
   medium-gauge floral wire
Small handful of Spanish moss
5 floral pins
72 floral picks

25 stems of fresh blue spruce,
   trimmed to 15 inches (39 cm.)
25 stems of fresh holly, trimmed to
   12 inches (30 cm.)
15 stems of lamb's ear, trimmed to
   12 inches
15 stems of heather trimmed, to
   12 inches
9 stems of silver king artemisia,
   trimmed to 8 inches (20 cm.)
9 stems of German statice, trimmed
   to 8 inches
9 stems of annual statice, trimmed
   to 8 inches

PROCEDURE

1. Make the arrangement's base by cutting the foam ball in
half with a serrated knife. Wire one half of the ball, flat side
down, to the bottom of a low basket. Cover the ball with
moss and secure in place with floral pins.
2. Prepare the blue spruce and holly by trimming the stems
at an angle. Attach each stem of lamb's ear to a single pick.
Create mini bouquets from the remaining materials, using
three stems per bouquet. Make five mini bouquets of heather,
three of silver king artemisia, three of German statice, and
three of annual statice. Attach all
mini bouquets to floral picks.
3. Create the shape of the
arrangement by inserting
stems of blue spruce, holly,
and lamb's ear into the foam
base. Fill out the arrangement by spacing the re-
maining materials evenly
around the base.

Herbal Tussie Mussie

Small enough to decorate
unusual places around the home,
herbal tussie mussies
embody the look and mood
of the Victorian era.

MATERIALS

Hot glue
Thin-gauge floral wire
Green floral tape
5-inch (12-cm.) cotton lace doily
Fabric stiffener
3 feet (180 cm.) of 1-inch
   (2.5-cm.) -wide gold ribbon
2 feet (120 cm.) of 1/4-inch
   (3/4-cm.)-wide green ribbon
2 feet of gold cord

7 stems of scented geranium leaves
5 stems of santolina
10 stems of tansy blooms
8 stems of rosemary
5 stems of Russian sage

PROCEDURE

1. Create seven mini bouquets from the herb materials listed
above in any combination. Each bouquet should contain five
stems.
2. Lengthen the stem portion of each mini bouquet to 4
inches (10 cm.) with floral wire and wrap with floral tape.
3. Cut a 1-inch hole in the center of the doily and dip the
doily in fabric stiffener.
4. Gather all of the mini bouquets together into one larger
bouquet. Push the stems of the bouquet through the hole.
Shape the doily around the outer edges of the bouquet and
allow it to dry before beginning the next step.
5. Secure the seven mini bouquet stems together by wrapping
them with floral tape. Cover the tape with gold
ribbon, securing as needed with
hot glue.
6. Make a bow from the gold
ribbon and wire it under the
doily. Last, create the
streamers by twisting a
4-inch length of floral wire
around the center point of the
green ribbon and the gold cord,
and then wiring them next to the bow.

GARLANDS, SWAGS
& HANGING BOUQUETS

At best, the lines of distinction between garlands, swags, and hanging bouquets are nebulous. The dictionary is of no help, and historical references only muddy the waters further. Circles of dried plants, called "garlands," have been excavated from 4000-year-old pyramids, while both short garlands and hanging bouquets have sometimes been referred to as "swags." Whatever name we choose to call them, most garlands, swags, and hanging bouquets are made from one of the several basic techniques explained below.

The projects on pages 98 and 102 were made by securing miniature bouquets of herbs to a long base with floral wire. These mini bouquets are positioned one at a time against the base and then attached by wrapping floral wire around their stems several times. Each new bouquet is positioned to cover the stems of the previous bouquet until the entire base is covered. Bases can be made from rope, macrame thread, or heavy-gauge floral wire.

The hanging bouquets on page 104 were made by arranging layers of herbs in a fan shape and then securing them together at the stems. The projects on pages 101 and 105 were made with two fan-shaped bouquets that were arranged so the stems of each bouquet would overlap. Bows were used to cover the overlapping stems in each project.

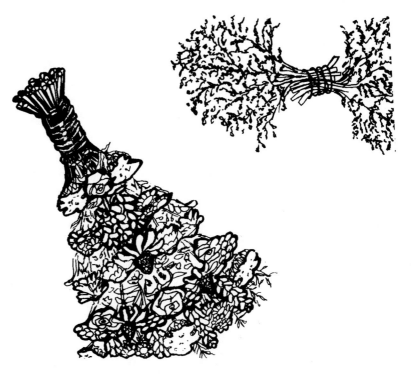

Custom-Shaped Garland

A flexible rope base enables the designer to custom-fit the garland around a kitchen window. The garland's colorful herbs—blue salvia and calendula—were chosen to complement a cherished collection of cobalt glass.

MATERIALS

12 feet (3 m.) of rope
1 spool of medium-gauge floral wire
Hot glue

90 stems of Italian oregano, trimmed to 6 inches
180 stems of silver king artemisia, trimmed to 6 inches (15 cm.)
120 stems of blue salvia, trimmed to 7 inches (17 cm.)
90 stems of Italian oregano, trimmed to 5 inches (12 cm.)
60 nigella seed heads
60 calendula blossoms
70 cornflowers
1 bulb of garlic

PROCEDURE

1. Working on a large table or other flat surface, assemble and wire 30 mini bouquets. Make each bouquet by layering three six-inch stems of Italian oregano on top of six stems of silver king artemisia. Then layer three stems of blue salvia on the artemisia, followed by three five-inch stems of Italian oregano. Secure each bouquet by wrapping the stems several times with floral wire. Last, hot-glue two nigella seed heads, two calendula blooms, and two cornflowers into each bouquet.

2. Mark the middle of the rope base. Position a single bouquet at one end of the rope, stems toward the middle, and secure with floral wire. Continue adding bouquets, positioning each to cover the stems of the previous bouquet, until the stems of the 15th bouquet overlap the middle mark of the rope.

3. Starting at the other end of the rope base, repeat step 2 with the remaining 15 bouquets.

4. Camouflage the stems of the two bouquets that meet at the center by hot-gluing stems of blue salvia and cornflowers over them. As a final touch, hot-glue a bulb of garlic in the center.

5. To hang the garland, position nails or tacks as desired and drape the garland over them.

GARLIC AND BAY KITCHEN GARLAND

If you love kitchen crafts, this garland of garlic, bay leaves, and colorful herb blooms will immediately win your heart. While the garland displays nicely in the traditional location over a door or window, it also looks lovely on a kitchen wall.

MATERIALS

12 × 36-inch (30 × 91-cm) piece of corrugated cardboard or 2-ply mount board
Hot glue

15 stems of bay leaves, trimmed to 3 inches (7 cm.)
36-inch length of braided garlic
40 globe amaranth blooms
60 bee balm blooms
8 strawflowers
20 stems of chamomile blooms, trimmed to 3 inches

PROCEDURE

1. Using a utility knife, cut a 3-inch-wide cardboard base for the garland.
2. Position the bay leaves along the bottom edge of the base and hot-glue in place.
3. Hot-glue the garlic braid to the base. Trim some of the stems from the end of the braid and hot-glue to the other end of the braid.
4. Hot-glue the globe amaranth, bee balm, and strawflowers randomly around the garlic.
5. Tuck the stems of chamomile under the garlic every 2 inches (5 cm.) and hot-glue in place.

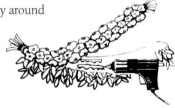

SILVER WALL SWAG

The strong horizontal shape of the wall swag shown on page 101 enables it to be easily transformed into a table centerpiece.

MATERIALS

Hot glue
6-inch (15-cm.) length of
medium-gauge floral wire
24 inches (60 cm.) of velvet
ribbon

6 stems of eucalyptus, trimmed to
36 inches (91 cm.)
20 stems of silver king artemisia,
trimmed to 16 inches (41 cm.)
6 stems of German statice, trimmed
to 14 inches (36 cm.)
10 stems of oregano blooms, trimmed
to 12 inches (30 cm.)

4 stems of sage, trimmed to
10 inches (25 cm.)
10 stems of chive blooms, trimmed
to 8 inches (20 cm.)
16 stems of blue salvia, trimmed
to 6 inches (15 cm.)

PROCEDURE

1. Create the arrangement's base by dividing the eucalyptus into two piles, each with three stems. Position the eucalyptus so that the stem ends overlap each other by about 1 inch (2-1/2 cm.). Secure the stems together with wire, but instead of trimming the leftover wire, shape it into a loop for hanging.

2. Arrange ten stems of silver king artemisia in a fan shape on each side of the swag. Tuck the stems under the wire and hot-glue for reinforcement.

3. Repeat step 2 with the German statice, oregano, sage, and chives, using half of the materials on each side.

4. Arrange eight stems of blue salvia on each side of the swag. Dab each stem with hot glue and tuck into the other herb materials.

5. Cut the ribbon into two lengths: one 18 inches and one 6 inches. Create a loop bow with the long length of ribbon. Use the short length of ribbon to fold around the center of the bow. Hot-glue to the center of the swag. (See pages 36-37 for bow-making instructions.)

Ambrosial Herbal Swag

The gentle contours of the fragrant herbal swag shown below enable it to display beautifully on a shelf, under a mantel, or over a doorway.

MATERIALS

1 54-inch (1-1/3-m.) length of medium-gauge floral wire
1 spool of thin-gauge floral wire
Hot glue
4 84-inch (2-m.) lengths of 1/8-inch (1/3-cm.) ribbon in complementary colors

40 stems of sweet Annie; 32 stems of lavender; 8 stems of white yarrow; 40 stems of rosemary; 8 stems of achillea 'The Pearl'; 32 stems of white sage; 16 stems of germander; 8 stems of goldenrod, cockscomb, miniature roses, and rue; 24 indigo spires; 40 stems of opal basil; 24 stems of anise hyssop; 16 stems of wormwood; 5 globe amaranth blooms without stems

Note: All materials (except the globe amaranth) should be trimmed to 5 inches (12 cm.)

PROCEDURE

1. Bend one end of the 54-inch wire back 3 inches (7 cm.) and twist it until you have a 1-inch loop. Repeat procedure on the other end. (The loops can be used to hang your finished swag.)

2. Working on a large table or other flat surface, create eight mini bouquets, each one containing five stems of sweet Annie, four stems of lavender, one stem of white yarrow, five stems of rosemary, one stem of achillea 'The Pearl,' and four stems of white sage.

3. With the remaining materials, create eight additional bouquets, each one containing: two stems of germander, one stem of goldenrod, one stem of cockscomb, one miniature rose, one stem of rue, three indigo spires, five stems of opal basil, three stems of anise hyssop, and two stems of wormwood.

4. Position the first bouquet against one end of the wire with the stems facing away from the loop. Secure the bouquet with thin-gauge floral wire. Continue securing bouquets to the wire base one at a time, alternating bouquet types and taking care that each new bouquet covers the stems of the previous bouquet. Position the globe amaranth blooms throughout the swag and hot-glue in place.

5. Holding the four ribbons together, gently wrap them around the swag in 8-inch (20-cm.) intervals and secure at each end by threading them through the wire loops and tying in knots. Allow any excess ribbon to remain if desired.

HERB DOLL BOUQUETS

With a few simple additions—miniature
straw hats, baskets, and bright ribbon streamers—
these hanging bouquets take on personalities
of their own. They can be made with
fresh or dried materials.

MATERIALS

For each doll:

1 large rubber band
1 miniature straw hat
1 corsage pin
1 miniature basket
2 or 3 2-1/2 foot lengths of assorted
ribbons

Herb materials for the doll shown left:

30 stems of sweet Annie, trimmed
to 18 inches (46 cm.)
Small handful assorted dried
blossoms

Herb materials for the doll shown right:

30 stems of the following herbs, in
any combination, trimmed
to 18 inches: sweet Annie,
purple sage, bee balm, Mexican
sage, Russian sage, larkspur,
blue salvia, scented geraniums,
daisies, rue, peppermint,
spearmint, thyme, fennel,
chamomile, catnip, yarrow,
coneflowers, and pennyroyal
Small handful assorted dried
blossoms

PROCEDURE

1. Arrange most of the herb stems until you have a fan shape
you find pleasing. Secure with a rubber band.
2. Tuck remaining stems under the rubber band one at a
time, and pull up to cover the
stems underneath. Trim the
stems even.
3. Tie the ribbons around the
rubber band. Use one length to
decorate the hat if desired.
4. Put the hat over the trimmed
stems and secure with the
corsage pin.
5. Fill the basket with dried
blossoms and tie the handle to
the end of one of the ribbons.

Door Swag

This small door swag makes a charming greeting when hung on the guest bedroom door, and the project is so easy to make that you may want to send the swag home with special guests. The bow can be removed and quickly exchanged with one of a new color.

MATERIALS

12-inch (30-cm.) vine wreath base
Hot glue
6-inch (15-cm.) length of medium gauge floral wire
Paper ribbon bow

16 stems of silver king artemisia, trimmed to 10 inches (25 cm.)
2 stems of sage, trimmed to 8 inches (20 cm.)

4 stems of oregano blooms, trimmed to 7 inches (17 cm.)
8 stems of chive blooms, trimmed to 6 inches
2 stems of lemon balm blooms, trimmed to 4 inches (10 cm.)
2 sprigs pepper berries
1 bee balm bloom

PROCEDURE

1. Prepare the swag's base by cutting a 12-inch vine wreath base in half. (Note: This will yield two swag bases.)
2. Position eight stems of silver king artemisia curving down each side of the base. Allow the stems to overlap slightly in the center and hot-glue in place.
3. Repeat step 2, dividing first the sage, then the oregano blooms, then the chive blooms, then the pepper berries, then the lemon balm.
4. Wire the bow to the swag at the point where the stems meet. Instead of cutting the wire, twist it into a loop for hanging.
5. Hot-glue a single bee balm bloom in the center of the bow.

WALL HANGINGS

Fragrant Broom Bouquet

If you love creating arrangements with herbs and flowers from your garden, but have simply run out of table space for displaying them, consider attaching an arrangement to a broom handle to create a beautiful wall hanging.

MATERIALS

Heavy-gauge floral wire
Hot glue
Country broom, approximately
    3 feet long (180 cm.)
3 feet of 3-inch (7-cm.) -wide cotton
    print ribbon

5 sprigs of 18-inch (1/6-cm.) sweet
    Annie
12 stems of silver king artemisia
5 stems of blue larkspur
4 stems of yarrow
7 stems of blue salvia
10 small bunches of mountain mint
7 stems of silver dollar eucalyptus

5 stems globe thistle
3 strawflowers
3 stems of gayfeather
10 coneflowers
1 cockscomb blossom

PROCEDURE

1. Working on a flat surface, arrange the sweet Annie sprigs to a width of about 8 inches (20 cm.) at the top and 1 inch (2-1/2 cm.) at the bottom. Next, add stems of silver king artemisia and blue larkspur to the sweet Annie background. Secure the stems together with heavy-gauge wire, taking care not to disturb the shape of the arrangement.

2. Position the clusters of yarrow, blue salvia, and mountain mint at different heights in the arrangement. (Note: you may need to lengthen some stems with floral wire; see page 31 for directions.) Secure the stems of these materials to the background arrangement with more heavy-gauge floral wire.

3. Using hot glue, add stems of silver dollar eucalyptus, globe thistle, strawflowers, gayfeather, coneflowers, and cockscomb throughout the arrangement.

4. Wire the arrangement to the broom. Using the cotton ribbon, tie a large bow around the base of the arrangement to prevent bare wires from showing.

Fragrant Summer Hat

Straw hats decorated with herbs and flowers have long been cherished by summer bridesmaids and garden party hostesses. When not being worn, display your decorated hats on a wall or door for year 'round enjoyment.

MATERIALS

Straw hat
Hot glue

Approximately 30 sprigs of sweet Annie, trimmed to 3 inches (7 cm.)
Approximately 20 blooms each of roses, crested cockscomb, strawflowers, and globe amaranth
Approximately 15 sprigs of curry plant, trimmed to 3 inches
Approximately 20 blooms each of blue salvia, lavender, sage leaves, annual statice
Approximately 15 sprigs each of baby's breath, silver king artemisia, and caspia, trimmed to 3 inches

PROCEDURE

1. Begin by framing the inner and outer circles of the hat's rim with sprigs of sweet Annie. Hot-glue the inner circle sprigs in an upright, vertical position, and glue the outer sprigs in a horizontal position, pointing toward the outer edge of the hat.
2. Working on the inner circle, arrange and hot-glue down the focal flowers by first placing a single large rose in the front, back, and on each side. Fill in the space next to the roses with large pieces of cockscomb and strawflowers.
3. Working on the outer circle, arrange the focal flowers by clustering three globe amaranth heads together in intervals of about three inches. Again, hot-glue them in place.
4. Fill in the space between the inner and outer circles with curry plant, blue salvia, lavender, sage, annual statice, globe amaranth, celosia, and smaller roses.
5. Last, add stems of baby's breath, silver king artemisia, and caspia to create an airy, delicate appearance.

POCKET BASKET ARRANGEMENT

Sharing the treasures of your garden with special friends is simple and inexpensive with small basket arrangements.

MATERIALS

8-inch (20-cm.) wall basket with a pocket
Small block of floral foam
5 floral pins
Hot glue

Moss
40 stems, in any combination, of beebalm blooms, black-eyed Susan blooms, love-in-a-mist seed heads, heather blooms, lamb's ear blooms, safflower blooms, comfrey foliage, Queen Anne's lace blooms, coneflower blooms, tarragon foliage, chamomile blooms, silver germander foliage, scented geranium foliage

PROCEDURE

1. With a serrated knife, cut a block of floral foam to fit the inside pocket of the basket and hot-glue in place. Cover any exposed areas of foam with moss and secure with floral pins.
2. Examine the stems of your materials. Separate them in two piles: one pile with stems sturdy enough to insert directly into the floral foam, and the other pile with delicate, weak stems. Cut the tips of all the sturdy stems at a sharp angle.
3. Starting at the back of the basket, begin inserting the stronger stems of blooms and foliage into the foam. Continue working toward the front of the basket, taking care to insert the stems slightly deeper into the foam as you get closer to the front. Stems bordering the rim of the basket should be flush with the basket.

4. Working with one stem at a time, apply a dab of hot glue to each delicate stem and position among the stronger-stemmed materials until you are pleased with the fullness of the arrangement.

Autumn Door Basket

A crescent-shaped arrangement of silver and gold herbs makes a perfect complement for the natural vine basket shown on page 111. The basket is narrow enough to fit in the thin space between an outside door and a storm door.

MATERIALS

Flat wall basket with a flat pocket
Paper bow
Hot glue

10 stems of silver king artemisia, trimmed to 9 inches (22 cm.)
8 stems of sweet Annie, trimmed to 7 inches (17 cm.)
3 stems of yarrow, trimmed to 3 inches (7 cm.)
4 stems of tansy blooms, trimmed to 3 inches
30 stems of feverfew, trimmed to 3 inches

PROCEDURE

1. Arrange the silver king artemisia in a crescent shape on one side of the basket and hot-glue in place. Arrange stems of sweet Annie on top of the artemisia and hot-glue.
2. Hot-glue the paper bow at the handle's base and arrange the loops to cover the artemisia and sweet Annie stems.
3. Hot-glue one stem of yarrow near the top and bottom of the bow, and another stem in the middle of the lower silver king artemisia spray.
4. Fill out the remaining space in the bouquet with stems of tansy and feverfew. To create a more natural look, hot-glue several stems of feverfew into the center of the bow.

Christmas Stocking

Celebrate the holiday season with this herbal wall hanging made with traditional colors. The fluffy texture of the stocking was created with short stems of ground pine and blooms of pearly everlasting. As with all natural materials you collect in the wild, be sure to harvest the ground pine with consideration for the environment.

MATERIALS

20 × 12-inch (50 × 30-cm.) rectangle of 1-inch (2-1/2-cm.) Styrofoam
90 wooden floral picks

18 stems of pearly everlasting, trimmed to 3 inches (7-1/2 cm.)
8 stems of globe amaranth blooms, trimmed to 2 inches (5 cm.)
10 stems of ground pine, trimmed to 3 inches
14 stems of sweet Annie, trimmed to 2 inches
10 stems of mountain mint, trimmed to 1 inch (2-1/2 cm.)

PROCEDURE

1. Trace a stocking shape onto the Styrofoam with a felt tip pen and cut it out with a serrated knife.
2. Attach all materials to floral picks, 1 stem per pick.
3. Beginning at the top of the stocking, insert three horizontal rows of pearly everlasting blooms, six picks to a row. Arrange the globe amaranth to fill in any bare spots.
4. Working in horizontal rows, cover the remaining surface area of the base with ground pine. The first row of pine should be tucked under the pearly everlasting.
5. Insert stems of sweet Annie and mountain mint throughout the ground pine. Arrange the ground pine tendrils to cover the edges of the stocking to cover unsightly foam.

SMALL GIFTS AND KEEPSAKES

HERBAL NAPKIN RINGS

While too delicate for everyday use, these napkin rings add the perfect touch to a special dining occasion.

MATERIALS

1 4-inch (10-cm.) grapevine wreath
1 piece of sheet moss
  Hot glue

4 sage leaves
4 sprigs of pepper berries
1 small rosebud
4 sprigs of baby's breath

4 chamomile buds
9 feverfew blooms
4 sprigs of cilantro seed heads
Note: This material list yields
1 decorated napkin ring

PROCEDURE

1. Prop the grapevine wreath against a solid item so you can decorate it in an upright position. Trim the sheet moss to an oval shape approximately 1-1/2 × 2-1/2 inches (4 × 6 cm.). Wrap the sheet moss around the top third of the base and hot-glue in place.

2. Begin decorating by hot-gluing four sage leaves, two to each side, in the center of the moss. Next, position a sprig of pepper berries on top of and toward the middle of each sage leaf and hot-glue in place.

3. Hot-glue a single rosebud in the center of the sage leaves, and then arrange and hot-glue the baby's breath in a starburst pattern in front of the rosebud.

4. Finish decorating by hot-gluing the chamomile, feverfew, and cilantro to the moss.

HERBAL BIRDHOUSE

With a thatched roof made from tiny lamb's ear leaves and other intricate herbal detailing, this indoor birdhouse will be the envy of every bird in the neighborhood.

MATERIALS

Wooden birdhouse (24 × 12 inches, 60 × 30 cm.)
Hot glue
Sheet moss
Small nails
10 twigs in various shapes
24-inch length of raffia
2-inch (5-cm.) miniature grapevine wreath base

300 lamb's ear leaves
180 yarrow stems (leaves and blossoms removed), trimmed to 3 inches (7 cm.)
72 rose hips
18 chamomile blooms
100 sprigs of accent materials (salvia, lavender, oregano, marjoram, anise, hyssop, larkspur, miniature roses)

PROCEDURE

1. Using hot glue, cover the sides, front, and back of the bird house with sheet moss. If desired, create a rustic look by nailing the twigs in horizontal and vertical positions around the house.

2. Hot-glue rows of lamb's ear to the roof until it's covered, using larger leaves on the bottom rows and progressively smaller leaves as you work upward. Position each leaf to slightly overlap the adjacent leaves.

3. Assemble the fence by hot-gluing lengths of yarrow stems together. Wrap the joints with raffia to cover the glue. (See illustration.) Then hot-glue the fence to the birdhouse's base.

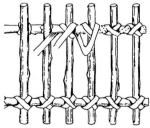

4. Hot-glue a rose hip to the top of each fence slat.

(Instructions continue on following page)

Herbal Birdhouse
(continued from previous page)

5. Create small points of interest by hot-gluing accent materials to the fence at the corners and half-way along the sides of the birdhouse.

6. Arrange the chamomile blooms around the wreath base and hot-glue in place. Then hot-glue the wreath to the opening of the birdhouse.

7. Use the remaining accent materials to embellish the roof by tucking them under the lamb's ear leaves and securing with hot glue. Concentrate the materials under the front eaves and decrease as you work toward the back.

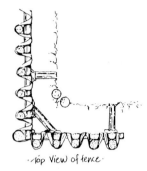

Top View of fence.

GLASS DOME

Simple finds at flea markets and dime-store sales magically transform into cherished collectibles and gifts when decorated with pressed herbs. The glass dome shown here was decorated in less than an hour, and enjoys a prominent position in an herbal crafter's bookcase.

MATERIALS

Glass dome, 10 inches (25 cm.) tall
White craft glue
Small paint brush
Aerosol resin

5 stems of fern
6 stems of delphinium blooms
2 stems of lavender geranium blooms
8 stems of red geranium blooms
5 stems of pink geranium blooms

PROCEDURE

1. Place all herb materials face down on a flat surface. Following the design indicated by the numbers in the illustration, apply a thin coat of glue to each flower or leaf with the paint brush and then gently press against the outside of the glass.

2. After the craft glue has dried completely (at least an hour), apply a thin coat of spray resin to protect the herbs.

Glass dome: (1) fern, (2) delphinium, (3) lavender geranium, (4) red geranium, (5) pink geranium

HERBAL TREE ORNAMENT

Transform an ordinary glass ornament into a magical showpiece in minutes by decorating it with small, colorful herbs.

MATERIALS

Glass tree ornament
White craft glue
Small paint brush
8-inch length of satin ribbon
Hot glue
Small satin loop bow (see
   pages 36-37 for bow-making
   instructions)

2 large dusty miller leaves
1 stem of celosia
2 stems of pepper berries, trimmed
   to 2 inches (5 cm.)
2 feverfew blooms

PROCEDURE

1. Place the dusty miller leaves face down on a flat surface. Working with one leaf at a time, paint the wrong side of the leaf with a thin layer of white craft glue. Gently position the leaves down each side of the ornament and press flat.

2. Form a loop with the eight-inch length of ribbon and hot-glue it to the top of the ornament. Next, hot-glue the bow over the ribbon ends, and then hot-glue a single celosia bloom into the center of the bow.

3. Position a single stem of pepper berries above each dusty miller leaf and hot-glue in place. Finish the ornament by hot-gluing a single feverfew bloom into the bow on the front and back sides.

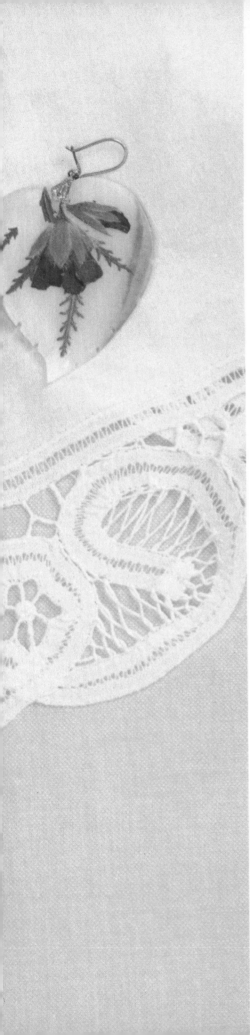

PRESSED HERB EARRINGS

Inexpensive mother-of-pearl earrings make one-of-a-kind gifts when decorated with pressed herbs and flowers.

MATERIALS

For earring at left:

1 pair of mother-of-pearl earrings
White craft glue
Small paint brush
Aerosol resin

2 small stems of dianthus foliage
6 pressed yarrow blooms
4 small stems of pressed lupine foliage

PROCEDURE

1. Arrange the blooms and foliage on the earrings to determine spacing.
2. Place all materials face down on a flat surface. Working first with the dianthus blooms, apply a thin coat of glue with the paint brush and then gently place against the outer side of each earring.
3. Repeat step 2 with the yarrow blooms and then the lupine foliage.
4. After the glue has dried completely (at least an hour), apply a thin coat of spray resin to protect the herbs.

MATERIALS

For earring at right:

1 pair of mother-of-pearl earrings
White craft glue
Small paint brush
Aerosol resin

8 small stems of pressed yarrow foliage
4 pressed geranium blooms

PROCEDURE

1. Arrange the blooms and foliage on the earrings to determine spacing.
2. Place all materials face down on a flat surface. Working first with the yarrow foliage, apply a thin coat of glue with the paint brush and then gently place against the outer side of each earring.
3. Repeat step 2 with the geranium blooms.
4. After the glue has dried completely (at least an hour), apply a thin coat of spray resin to protect the herbs.

JOB'S-TEARS NECKLACE

Seeds from Job's-tears, an ornamental grass, make lovely jewelry and have been associated with luck and protection for hundreds of years.

MATERIALS

Needle
20-inch length (50-cm.) of nylon thread or fishing line
Purchased metal jewelry clasp

75 Job's-tears seeds

PROCEDURE

1. Harvest the seeds after they have matured and changed from their immature green color.
2. Thread the needle and work each seed down over the needle until your necklace is the desired length. (The seeds are naturally hollow so you will not have to pierce them with the needle or drill holes.)
3. Apply the jewelry clasp per the instructions on the package.

GIFT BOOKS

Decorating the pages of diaries and albums with pressed herbs transforms an ordinary gift into a special keepsake. To make the gift more memorable, use herbs with historical meanings appropriate to the occasion, and enclose a small card explaining their symbolism.

MATERIALS

For the diary, left:

Diary, wedding album, or baby book
White craft glue
Small paint brush
Aerosol resin

3 stems of asparagus fern
6 red geranium blooms
6 pink geranium blooms

PROCEDURE

1. Place all herb materials face down on a flat surface. Following the design indicated by the numbers in the illustration below, apply a thin coat of glue to each flower or leaf with the paint brush and gently press against the paper.
2. After the craft glue has dried completely (at least an hour), apply a thin coat of spray resin to protect the herbs.

Diary page: (1) asparagus fern, (2) red geranium, (3) pink geranium

REFRIGERATOR MAGNETS

Wooden cutouts decorated with small stems of pressed herbs and greenery make a fun project to produce in bulk for fundraising bazaars or to entertain children on a rainy afternoon. The cutouts can also be drilled at the top, threaded with gold ribbon, and used as tree ornaments during the holidays.

For the red heart:
  4 small stems of fern
  3 helianthemum blooms
  1 carnation bloom

For the white heart:
  3 small stems of fern
  4 geranium blooms
  4 delphinium blooms

For the pineapple:
  7 small stems of fern
  10 geranium blooms

MATERIALS

Wooden cutouts in shapes and colors of your choice
White craft glue
Small paint brush
Aerosol resin

PROCEDURE

1. Place all herb materials face down on a flat surface. Apply a thin coat of glue to each flower or leaf with the paint brush and then gently press against the wood.
2. After the craft glue has dried completely (at least an hour), apply a thin coat of spray resin to protect the herbs.

SPICY CENTERPIECE

A colorful potpourri of herbs and natural materials hot-glued to a foam ring creates this fragrant table decoration.

MATERIALS

5-inch (12-cm.) foam ring
Brown floral tape
Hot glue

50 whole cloves
30 bay leaves
10 sage leaves
 4 sprigs of oregano blooms
 5 sprigs of juniper berries
 8 sprigs of yarrow
 4 sprigs of tansy

 8 sprigs of lemon grass
 5 sprigs of pepper berries
 7 sprigs of feverfew
 5 small chili peppers
 4 star anise
 8 small cinnamon sticks
10 pumpkin seeds

PROCEDURE

1. Cover the foam base with brown floral tape by wrapping it at 1/4-inch (2/3-cm.) intervals.
2. Decorate the outer sides of the base with two rows of cloves. *Note:* Although you can attach the cloves with hot glue, they adhere much faster by simply pushing the pointed ends through the tape and into the foam.
3. Using hot glue, cover the top of the base with bay leaves, positioning them so their tips face outward.
4. Hot-glue the remaining materials to the bay leaves.

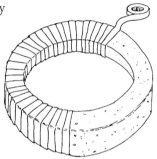

DECORATED CLIPBOARD

Since handcrafted wood items are a favorite
of so many herbal crafters, it seems only natural
to showcase the beauty of both arts together.
In this project, the top of a metal clip is
embellished with herbs for a lovely result.

MATERIALS

Clipboard (6 × 10 inches,
    15 × 25 cm.)
Thin-gauge floral wire
Hot glue

8 stems of dusty miller
8 stems of silver king artemisia
2 stems of oregano blooms
2 stems of tansy blooms
2 stems of feverfew blooms
4 small cinnamon sticks
1 large chive blossom

Note: All materials trimmed to
2-inch (5-cm.) lengths

PROCEDURE

1. Arrange two mini bouquets, each one containing four
stems of dusty miller, four stems of silver king artemisia, one
stem of oregano blooms, one stem of
tansy blooms, one stem of
feverfew blooms, and two
cinnamon sticks. Secure each
bouquet with wire.
2. Wire both bouquets to the
metal clip with stem ends facing
the center.
3. Cover the bouquets' stems by
hot-gluing a large chive blossom in
the center.

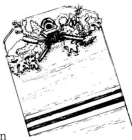

CURTAIN TIEBACK

Accentuate the wispy texture
of country lace curtains with a
custom-designed herbal curtain tieback.

MATERIALS

4-inch (10-cm) grapevine
wreath base
1 spool of floral wire
Hot glue
2 yards (1-3/4 m.) narrow green
velvet ribbon

12 stems of dusty miller, trimmed to
4 inches
3 chive blossoms
4 dill seed heads
10 larkspur blossoms
3 miniature pine cones
1 cornflower

Note: To make a pair of curtain
tiebacks, simply double the
materials.

PROCEDURE

1. Cut the vine base in half. Make two hooks from floral wire
and hot glue one hook to each open end of the base.
2. Arrange the dusty miller into three mini bouquets (four
stems to a bouquet).
3. Hold a single bouquet of dusty miller against the base
(about two inches, five cm., up from one end) and secure by
wrapping several times with floral wire. Position the next
bouquet over the stems of the first bouquet and again secure
with wire. Attach the next two bunches in the same way.
4. Starting at one end of the base, begin wrapping the velvet
ribbon around the grape vine, overlapping it to prevent gaps
and hot-gluing as necessary. After you've covered the first
bouquet of dusty miller stems, wrap the
ribbon loosely in 1-inch (2-1/2-cm.)
intervals. When you've passed
the dusty miller foliage, begin
overlapping the ribbon again,
hot-gluing as needed.

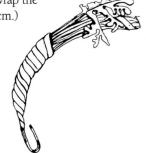

5. Hot-glue the chive blossoms, larkspur, dill seed heads,
pine cones, and the cornflower
into the dusty miller.

GATHERING WILD MATERIALS

Gathering herbs and wildflowers on roadsides,
fields, and forests can be a wonderful experience, but the environmental implications
should never be ignored. Pick only a few of
each type of plant, never pull up plants by
their roots, and always use an identification
book to ensure you don't pick endangered or
threatened species.

A list of endangered and threatened plants
can be found in the Code of Federal Regula-
tions (CFR), under Title 50, Part 17, Section
12. You can secure a copy of this list at most
university and large public libraries, or call your
local or state office of the U.S. Fish and Wildlife Service. Although the federal office of the
Fish and Wildlife Service is not equipped to
handle massive inquiries, you may write to
them for a copy of the list at the address below
after you've exhausted other possibilities.

Research Publications
130ARLSQ
U.S. Fish and Wildlife Service
Department of Interior
1849 C Street, N.W.
Washington, DC 20240

HERBAL TABLE TREE

Made from a simple cone-shaped base, this herb tree makes a lovely complement to handcrafted miniatures or other cherished collectibles. For the holiday season, display the tree with a bowl of colorful Christmas ornaments.

MATERIALS

12-inch (30-cm.) foam cone
123 wooden floral picks

32 stems of yarrow, trimmed to
4 inches (10 cm.)
7 stems of bee balm, trimmed to
2 inches
15 stems of echinops, trimmed to
2 inches
10 stems of santolina, trimmed to
4 inches
20 stems of lamb's ear, trimmed
to 5 inches
8 stems of nigella, trimmed to
2 inches (5 cm.)
20 stems of peppermint, trimmed to
5 inches (12 cm.)
40 stems of silver king artemisia,
trimmed to 5 inches
48 stems of German statice,
trimmed to 5 inches
40 stems of lavender, trimmed to
5 inches

PROCEDURE

1. Attach the yarrow, bee balm, echinops, santolina, and lamb's ear to floral picks, 1 stem per pick.
2. Attach the following materials to picks in bundles of four stems per pick: nigella, peppermint, silver king artemisia, German statice, and lavender.
3. Cover the top and bottom areas of the cone with yarrow. Insert any remaining stems of yarrow intermittently around the cone.
4. Insert the nigella, bee balm, peppermint, echinops, and santolina randomly around the base.
5. Fill in remaining areas with silver king artemisia, German statice, lavender, and lamb's ear. Remember to insert the lamb's ear last because it's so easily damaged.

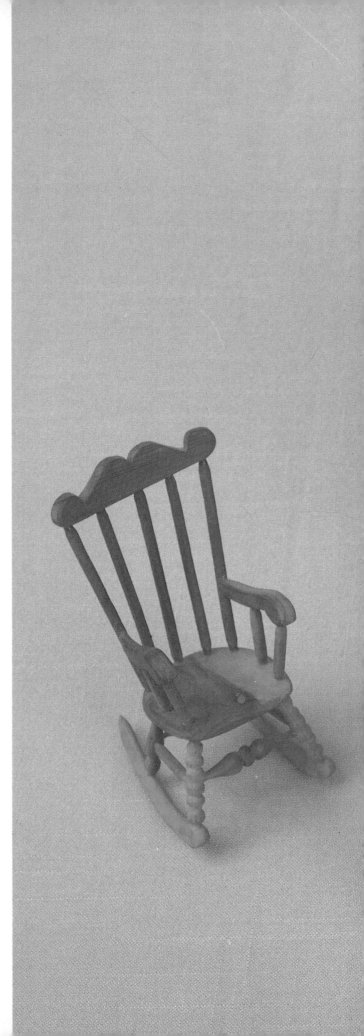

FRAGRANCE FAVORITES

Lavender Bottle Sachet

Lavender bottles are a wonderful way to preserve the beauty and fragrance of your lavender blooms. Use them to embellish gift packages, scent lingerie drawers, or decorate tabletops. When house guests are expected, place a lavender bottle between their sheets for a special welcome.

MATERIALS

1 spool of green sewing thread
1 18-inch (46-cm.) length of 1/8-inch (1/3-cm.) double-faced satin ribbon
1 4-foot (120-cm.) length of 1/8-inch double-faced satin ribbon

13 stems of lavender

PROCEDURE

1. Cut 13 stems of lavender when the lower blossoms have just begun to open. Although you will want the stems to be as long as possible, do not cut below this year's growth. To make the stems easier to work with, place your fresh-cut lavender in a glass of water and refrigerate them for at least 24 hours but not longer than one week.

2. Remove your stems from the refrigerator and line them up

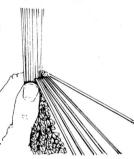

on a flatsurface with the flower heads even. Trim the stems to even lengths. Keeping the heads even, gather the stems into a bouquet and secure them together by wrapping with sewing thread just below the heads. Secure them a second time 1/2 inch (1-1/4 cm.) below the first thread.

3. Holding the bouquet upside down just below the second thread with your left hand, gently bend the stems down and over the thread one at a time. The result will look like a half-opened umbrella frame and the lavender blossoms will be caged inside the stems.

4. Tie one end of the 4-foot satin ribbon around the lavender bottle at the point where the blossoms end (called the "neck" of the lavender bottle) and thread the other end of the ribbon through a tapestry needle. Weave the ribbon in and out through the stems, occasionally pulling the ribbon taut to prevent twisting.

5. When you reach the top of the lavender bottle, tie a knot at the end of the ribbon and tuck it into the stems. Tie the 18-inch length of ribbon around the bottle's neck and spiral it down the stems, finishing in a bow. Hang the finished lavender bottle in a dry place for approximately ten days.

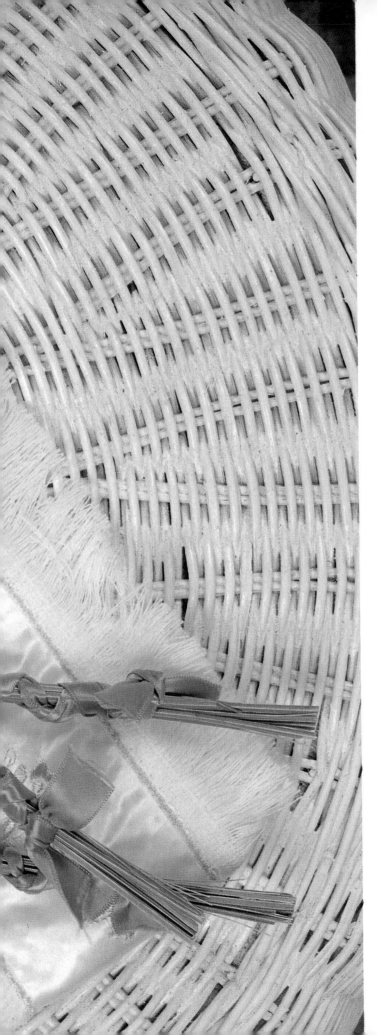

LAVENDER STICKS

For a quick gift that even children can make,
try tying bright ribbon around stems of lavender.
The lavender sticks can then be displayed
in a tall vase or used to add fragrance
in linen and clothing drawers.

MATERIALS

1 30-inch (75-cm.) length of satin ribbon

8 to 10 stems of lavender, trimmed to 14 inches (36 cm.)

Note: Since the ribbon covers most of the lavender, this project is an ideal way to use lavender with small imperfections.

PROCEDURE

1. Assemble eight to ten stems of lavender in a bunch and trim their stems even.
2. Fold the ribbon in half and place the center point over the top of the lavender.
3. Work the ribbon down the lavender stick by overlapping the two lengths every 1/2-inch (1-1/4 cm.).
4. Secure the ends by tying in three successive knots.

CREATIVE POTPOURRIS

For an herb gardener, collecting the small leaves, stems,
and blooms that make up a potpourri is an exciting process
that often leads to the invention of new potpourri recipes. An
herbal potpourri may feature vibrant colors, interesting textures, an
enchanting fragrance, or a combination of all three.

If your goal is to create potpourris for display in bowls around your home, you
need only combine the materials until you're satisfied with the quantity and

attractiveness of your potpourri. If fragrance is your goal, you have several options. The method of preference for many herbal crafters is to simply include fragrant herbs in their potpourri's recipe. The fragrance in these types of potpourris is generally strong, but not so intense that it consumes an entire room. Natural fragrances can be freshened every few months by adding additional fragrant herbs, or they can be "fixed" by adding a teaspoon (5 ml.) of crushed orrisroot for every cup (225 ml.) of potpourri.

Recipes for potpourris illustrated. Top: Equal amounts of globe thistle, lamb's ear, globe amaranth, silver king artemisia, strawflowers, and wild moss. **Bottom:** Equal amounts of wild grass, bee balm, strawflowers, and dianthus. **Left:** Equal amounts of lemon balm, lemon verbena, annual statice, strawflowers, and calendula. (*Note:* This potpourri also makes a fragrant simmer; just bring one cup of the potpourri to a boil in a small pan of water and then reduce heat.) **Right:** Equal amounts of hydrangea, Queen Anne's lace, calendula, basil, and globe thistle.

SWEATER SACHETS

Reminiscent of Victorian traditions,
these lace doily sachets add a romantic touch
to ordinary sweater drawers and closets.
For the more practical-minded,
moth-repelling pennyroyal is an
ingredient in each sachet's potpourri.

MATERIALS

For sachet at right:

8-inch (20 cm.) cotton lace doily
7-inch (17-cm.) circle of tulle
Hot glue
2 18-inch (46-cm.) lengths of
narrow ribbon

1 rosebud
6 stems lamb's ear, trimmed to
4 inches (10 cm.)
8 stems peppermint, trimmed
to 4 inches
8 stems wormwood, trimmed to
4 inches
8 stems German statice, trimmed
to 4 inches
1/2 cup (.12 liter) potpourri

POTPOURRI RECIPE

Equal amounts of peppermint and pennyroyal.

PROCEDURE

1. Place potpourri in the center of the tulle circle and fold in half. Secure around the edges with hot glue.
2. Fold the lace doily in half and slip the tulle-covered potpourri inside.
3. Weave one length of the ribbon through the outside edges of the doily to secure the potpourri pouch inside.
4. Make a small looped bow (see pages 36 and 37 for directions) with the other length of ribbon and hot-glue it to the top of the doily.
5. Create the center of the arrangement by first hot-gluing the rosebud to the center of the bow. Then hot-glue a single lamb's ear leaf on each side of the rose.
6. Fill out the arrangement by hot-gluing stems of peppermint, wormwood, lamb's ear, and German statice around the arrangement.

(Instructions continue on following page)

POTPOURRI BAGS

Decorated potpourri bags are an ideal way to use up scrap pieces of both fabric and herbs, and add a decorative touch to gift packages.

MATERIALS

For sachet at left on page 139:

> 6-inch (15-cm.) lace doily
> 5-inch (12-cm.) circle of tulle
> 2 18-inch (46-cm.) lengths of narrow ribbon

> 8 stems santolina, trimmed to 4 inches (10 cm.)
> 8 stems yarrow foliage, trimmed to 4 inches
> 8 stems feverfew, trimmed. to 4 inches
> 12 clover heads
> 1/2 cup (.12 liter) potpourri

MATERIALS

> 1 small piece of fabric cut to 12 inches wide × 11 inches long (30 × 27 cm.)
> 12-inch length of satin ribbon

> 2 stems silver king artemisia, trimmed to 4 inches (10 cm.)
> 10 small accent herbs (the bag on the top uses feverfew, larkspur, and peppermint leaves, while the bag on the bottom uses globe amaranth and sage leaves)
> 1-1/2 cups (340 ml.) of potpourri

POTPOURRI RECIPE

Equal amounts of rose petals, yarrow, cinnamon sticks, cloves, feverfew, peppermint, lavender, santolina, and pennyroyal.

POTPOURRI RECIPE

Equal amounts of peppermint, spearmint, and tansy.

PROCEDURE

1. Place potpourri in the center of the tulle circle and fold in half. Secure around the edges with hot glue.
2. Fold the lace doily in half and slip the tulle-covered potpourri inside.
3. Weave one length of the ribbon through the outside edges of the doily to secure the potpourri pouch inside.
4. Make a small looped bow (see pages 36 and 37 for directions) with the other length of ribbon and hot-glue it to the top of the doily.
5. Create the center of the arrangement by first hot-gluing stems of santolina, yarrow, and feverfew under the bow and radiating outward. Last, arrange the clover heads around the arrangement and hot-glue in place.

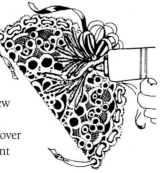

PROCEDURE

1. Fold the fabric in half, right sides together, to form a rectangle 6 × 11 inches (15 × 27 cm.). Sew the side seams. Turn right side out, fold the top down 2 inches (5 cm.) inside the bag, and press with a hot iron. Fill with potpourri and tie the bag closed with ribbon.
2. Arrange the two stems of silver king artemisia to form a crescent shape and hot-glue them to the ribbon. (The two stems should overlap about 1/2 inch, 1-1/4 cm.)
3. Hot-glue the foliage stems (sage or peppermint) into the silver king artemisia.
4. Create a small cluster of accent blooms (globe amaranth or feverfew and larkspur) in the center of the arrangement and hot-glue in place.

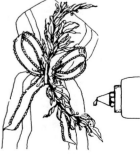

BATH BAG

Long renowned for their abilities to soothe and comfort the skin, sachets of comfrey and chamomile potpourri make welcome bath companions. The bag can be used as a body sponge or tied under the bathtub's faucet.

MATERIALS

1 7-inch (17-cm.) square piece of muslin or other light fabric
12-inch (30-cm.) length of ribbon or string
1 cup (225 ml.) potpourri

POTPOURRI RECIPE

Equal amounts of comfrey and chamomile.

PROCEDURE

Place the potpourri in the center of the fabric square. Gather all edges of fabric over the potpourri and tie with ribbon or string.

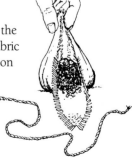

SPICY HERBAL POMANDERS

Decorated with delicate herb sprigs,
these easy-to-make pomander balls make
beautiful tree ornaments, package decorations,
and miniature air fresheners.

MATERIALS

Hot glue
Prepared pomander balls
(see recipe at right)

6 stems of herbs (santolina, peppermint leaves, and comfrey blooms for the pomander on the left; bittersweet, peppermint leaves, and feverfew blooms for pomander in the center; lamb's ear and peppermint for the pomander on the right), trimmed to 1-1/2 inches (4 cm.)

PROCEDURE

Working with one stem at a time, position three herbs under each side of the pomander's ribbon and secure with hot glue.

POMANDER RECIPE

Ingredients:
- 1/2 cup (110 ml.) ground cinnamon
- 3 tablespoons (15 ml.) ground allspice
- 3 tablespoons ground cloves
- 2 tablespoons (10 ml.) ground nutmeg
- 2 tablespoons orrisroot powder
- 1 cup (220 ml.) applesauce

Additional Materials:
- 12 12-inch (30-cm.) lengths of thin ribbon

Procedure:

1. Combine the first five ingredients and mix well. Stir in the applesauce, blending well.

2. Mold the dough into 12 balls, each one about the size of a walnut. Fold a 12-inch length of ribbon in half and push the ends of the ribbon through the center of each ball with a small crochet hook and mold dough around the ribbon.

3. Place the balls on a metal tray to dry and turn them once a day for five to ten days.

Note: Do not decorate pomanders until they have dried.

RUSTIC POTPOURRI

Depending on the ingredients in your recipe, an herbal potpourri can be as delicate or as rustic as you choose.

POTPOURRI RECIPE

Mix equal amounts of sumac, chestnuts, iris seed heads, and juniper berries until you have the quantity desired. Next, add small pieces of cinnamon sticks, cloves, star anise, and nutmeg until you have a pleasing fragrance.

CULINARY CRAFTS

CRYSTALLIZED CONFECTIONS

Crystallized leaves and blossoms are simple to make, yet add a magical mood to everyday entertaining and special events. While sage, mint, and violets were used for this display, the same recipe works on other edibles such as lemon balm leaves and rose petals.

INGREDIENTS

1 egg white
1 teaspoon water
50 sage and peppermint leaves
50 violet, borage, or Johnny jump-up blossoms
1/2 cup granulated sugar

PROCEDURE

1. Separate the egg and thin the egg white with one teaspoon of water. Spread the leaves and blossoms in a single layer on a sheet of wax paper.

2. Using a small pastry brush, dampen each leaf and blossom with the egg white mixture.

3. Sprinkle them with sugar and allow to dry for at least a day before serving. Leftovers can be stored for up to a month in the refrigerator.

WILD MINT TEA

For tea connoisseurs, inventing new tea recipes with your garden's culinary herbs will soon become a favorite pastime. The recipe below is made in bulk from dried herbs so you can enjoy the tea year 'round or package it in small portions as gifts.

RECIPE

Combine 1 cup each of lemon balm and spearmint leaves, 1/2 cup of orange mint leaves, and 4 tablespoons of grated orange peel. For each serving of tea, pour one cup of boiling water over one to two teaspoons of herb blend. Allow to steep for 20 to 30 minutes. Re-heat or serve iced. For a spicier variation, add one or two small cloves to steeping tea.

BEE BALM TEA

Revered by early American Indians and colonists as a medicinal herb, bee balm blooms are still enjoyed today in flavorful teas. A member of the mint family, bee balm's blooms come in vibrant purples and magentas as well as pastel shades.

RECIPE

Place one or two dried bee balm blooms in each cup. Fill cups with boiling water, steep five to seven minutes, and strain. Sweeten if desired. Serve hot or cold.

CHAMOMILE TEA

While it's still unknown whether chamomile's reputation for calming nerves is based on fact, the delicious apple and lemon flavors are relaxing in themselves.

RECIPE

Place one teaspoon of dried chamomile flowers (stems removed) in each cup. Add boiling water, allow to steep five to ten minutes, and strain. Sweeten with sugar or honey if desired.

VIOLET SYRUP

Served over waffles, pancakes, or vanilla ice cream, violet syrup is another way to enjoy the delicate flavor and beauty of fresh violets.

INGREDIENTS

Violet blossoms
Boiling water
Lemon juice
Granulated sugar

PROCEDURE

1. Fill glass jars (any size) with freshly harvested violet blossoms. Cover the violets with boiling water, cover the jars, and allow them to infuse for 24 hours.
2. Drain the violets and measure the infusion liquid. To each cup of liquid, add the juice of half a lemon and two cups of sugar. Bring the mixture to a boil, pour into sterilized jars or bottles, and seal.

VIOLET JAM

Rich in the characteristic flavor and color of fresh violets, violet jam is a delicacy to be savored in small amounts. The jam freezes well, making it an ideal gift from the garden during the holiday season.

INGREDIENTS

1-1/2	cups water
	Juice of 1 medium-sized lemon
1	cup firmly packed violet blossoms
2-1/2	cups sugar
1	3-ounce package powdered pectin

PROCEDURE

1. In an electric blender or food processor, blend 3/4 cup of water, the lemon juice, and the violet blossoms until the mixture resembles a smooth paste. Slowly add 2-1/2 cups of sugar and blend until dissolved.

2. In a small saucepan stir the powdered pectin into 3/4 cup of water and boil for one minute. Pour into the violet blossom mixture and blend about one minute. Quickly pour into small sterilized glass jars and seal.

3. After the jam has cooled, keep it in the refrigerator for three weeks or store it for up to a year in the freezer.

ROSE GERANIUM COOKIES

Rose geranium cookies make a delightful treat
for guests and are a fun way to share
the fruits of your garden.

INGREDIENTS

1/2 cup butter
1 cup sugar
1 egg
1/2 cup milk
1 teaspoon rose water
2 teaspoons rose geranium leaves, finely
chopped
2-1/2 cups flour
1-1/2 teaspoons baking powder
4 dozen small rose geranium leaves for
garnish

PROCEDURE

1. Cream butter and sugar together until light and fluffy. Beat in egg, milk, and rose water.
2. Sift together dry ingredients and add them, together with the chopped leaves, to the creamed mixture, stirring until well mixed.
3. Drop by heaping teaspoons onto lightly greased cookie sheet and press a single rose geranium leaf deep into each cookie.
4. Preheat oven to 350º (178º C) and bake for eight to ten minutes. Serve with a gentle companion such as bee balm tea.

HERBAL DESSERT SAUCE

Although culinary herbs are often associated with recipes for meats and vegetables, their unique flavors are wonderful enhancements to sweet fruits, pastries, and compotes.

INGREDIENTS

1/3 cup heavy cream
3/4 cup buttermilk
1 teaspoon grated lemon rind
1/4 teaspoon ground ginger
1/8 teaspoon ground cardamom
1/4 teaspoon garam masala, allspice, or nutmeg

PROCEDURE

1. Whip the cream in a medium-sized, chilled bowl until soft peaks form.
2. Mix remaining ingredients together in a small bowl and gently fold into the cream. The sauce should be the consistency of thick cream.

Note: For a thicker sauce, use only 1/4 cup of buttermilk.

A sliver of crystallized ginger adds a flavorful accent to a display of baked pears served on top of the herbal dessert sauce.

HERBAL VINEGARS

Few gifts are more warmly received and more passionately enjoyed than an herbal crafter's vinegars. And while traditional tarragon and garlic vinegars are always popular, you may want to try combining several of your favorite herbs for more unique-tasting vinegars that make wonderful marinades or salad dressings.

JT'S SOUTHWEST VINEGAR

Ingredients:

> 8 cups dry basil leaves and blooms (no stems)
> 2 heads peeled garlic cloves
> 10 dried red peppers
> 1 gallon red wine vinegar

CHEF'S BLEND VINEGAR

Ingredients:

> 4 cups dry rosemary
> 4 cups dry basil leaves and blooms (no stems)
> 30 stems of marjoram trimmed to 6 inches (15 cm.)
> 2 heads peeled garlic cloves
> 3 tablespoons crushed red pepper
> 1 gallon red wine vinegar

PROCEDURE

1. Put all the ingredients called for in the recipe of your choice, except the vinegar, in a one-gallon glass jar.

2. Heat the vinegar in a non-aluminum pot—but do not boil—and pour about half over the herb mixture.

3. Crush and bruise the herbs with a wooden spoon to release their flavor into the vinegar. Top off the jar with the remaining vinegar.

4. Cover the glass jar with a non-metallic lid and store in a cool, dry place for two weeks. Strain the vinegar and pour into display bottles. Add sprigs of fresh herbs to each bottle for visual interest if desired.

MAYONNAISE SAUCE

Mayonnaise is a wonderful vehicle for the taste of fresh herbs. Chives, parsley, basil, dill, fennel, and tarragon all work well, and a more intense flavor can be created by adding a clove of fresh garlic or a few drops of hot chili oil.

INGREDIENTS

1 cup mayonnaise
1 teaspoon fresh dill, finely chopped
1 teaspoon fresh parsley, finely chopped
1 garlic clove, finely chopped
1 teaspoon ginger root, finely grated
1 tablespoon lemon juice

PROCEDURE

Mix all ingredients together and store in refrigerator until ready for use.

BASIC HERBAL BUTTER

Herbal butters make versatile, flavorful garnishes that can be served on a variety of foods. Add your favorite garden herbs to the basic recipe below to create your own special recipes.

INGREDIENTS

4 tablespoons unsalted butter, softened
1 to 2 tablespoons fresh herbs, finely chopped
(or 1 teaspoon dried herbs and a dash of pepper)

PROCEDURE

1. Beat the softened butter until creamy. Blend in the chopped herbs.
2. Place the butter on waxed paper and form it into a roll or other shape with a flat-bladed knife. (A pastry bag can be used to create more intricate shapes.)
3. Allow the butter to "rest" in the refrigerator for at least two hours so the butter will completely absorb the flavor of the herbs.

Note: For an elegant touch, reserve some fresh herbs to decorate the top of the butter before serving.

TARRAGON BUTTER

This herbal butter makes a flavorful complement to fresh grilled salmon.

INGREDIENTS

4 tablespoons unsalted butter, softened
1 tablespoon fresh tarragon, finely chopped
1 tablespoon fresh dill, finely chopped
1 teaspoon powdered bay leaves
1 teaspoon lemon pepper

PROCEDURE

1. Beat the softened butter until creamy. Blend in remaining ingredients.
2. Place the butter on waxed paper and form it into a roll or other shape with a flat-bladed knife. (A pastry bag can be used to create more intricate shapes.)
3. Allow the butter to "rest" in the refrigerator for at least two hours so the butter will completely absorb the flavor of the herbs.

ROSE PETAL BUTTER

A colorful herbal butter made from rose petals
is a wonderful way to share the exquisite
taste of roses with special guests.

INGREDIENTS

4 tablespoons unsalted butter, softened
1-1/2 tablespoons fresh rose petals, finely chopped

PROCEDURE

1. Beat the softened butter until creamy. Blend in the
chopped rose petals.
2. Place the butter on waxed paper and form it into a roll or
other shape with a flat-bladed knife. (A pastry bag can be used
to create more intricate shapes.)
3. Allow the butter to "rest" in the refrigerator for at least two
hours so the butter will completely absorb the flavor of the
rose petals.

HERB AND SPICE BUTTER

The basic herbal butter recipe on page 161 can easily be doubled so there's enough to spread over lamb chops during grilling and to serve with the meal for baked potatoes, steamed vegetables, and rolls.

INGREDIENTS

8 tablespoons unsalted butter, softened
2 tablespoons fresh rosemary, finely chopped
1 tablespoon fresh tarragon, finely chopped
1 tablespoon fresh chives, finely chopped
1 tablespoon curry powder

PROCEDURE

1. Beat the softened butter until creamy. Blend in remaining ingredients.
2. Place the butter on waxed paper and form it into a roll or other shape with a flat-bladed knife. (A pastry bag can be used to create more intricate shapes.)
3. Allow the butter to "rest" in the refrigerator for at least two hours so the butter will completely absorb the flavor of the herbs.

PESTO

As any pesto aficionado knows, pesto is easy to make and always a crowd pleaser. Although traditionally served with pasta, pesto is equally enjoyable when stirred into hot rice, baked into bread, folded into an omelet, or served with fresh tomato slices.

INGREDIENTS

3 cups loosely packed fresh basil leaves
1/2 cup loosely packed fresh parsley leaves
2 to 3 large garlic cloves, peeled
1 tablespoon butter
1/2 cup pine nuts
1 cup olive oil
1-1/2 cups freshly grated Parmesan cheese

PROCEDURE

1. Mince the basil and parsley leaves in a food processor. Remove and set aside.
2. Mince the garlic cloves and leave in the food processor.
3. Melt the butter over low heat in a small skillet. Add the pine nuts and toast for one to two minutes, stirring often.
4. Pour the butter and pine nuts into the food processor and mince with the garlic.
5. Place the minced basil and parsley back in the food processor and blend together with the garlic and pine nuts mixture. Drizzle the olive oil into the mixture as it's being blended.
6. Transfer the entire mixture to a medium-sized bowl and stir in the cheese.

Note: Pesto freezes well if you cover it with a thin film of olive oil to prevent it from drying out.

HERBAL VEGETABLE DRESSING

Finding a salad dressing that will enhance the fresh, natural flavors of garden vegetables—instead of disguising them, as many commercially prepared dressings do—is a challenge most chefs enjoy. The basic recipe below is as delicious on cold vegetables as it is on hot ones, and you should feel free to add your own favorite herbs.

INGREDIENTS

1/2 teaspoon fresh parsley
1/2 teaspoon fresh tarragon
1/2 teaspoon fresh chives
1/2 teaspoon fresh chervil
3 tablespoons wine vinegar
9 tablespoons olive oil (virgin or extra virgin)
1 teaspoon Dijon mustard
1/2 teaspoon salt
1/2 teaspoon freshly ground black pepper

PROCEDURE

1. Mince the fresh herbs, reserving a few leaves to use as garnishes.
2. Place all ingredients in a small mixing bowl. Beat vigorously with a wire whisk until well blended.
3. Garnish with fresh leaves and serve immediately.

Winter Squash Baking Sauce

INGREDIENTS

2 tablespoons melted butter
1 tablespoon chervil
1 tablespoon sage
1 tablespoon ginger
1 tablespoon honey

Baking your next winter squash with this sauce will fill your kitchen with the wonderful fragrance of fresh herbs and spices.

PROCEDURE

1. Combine all ingredients.
2. Cut a winter squash (acorn, banana, buttercup, butternut, hubbard, spaghetti, or turk's turban) in half and scoop out the seeds.
3. Spoon the sauce into the center of each squash half and bake as usual.

Lemon Balm Bread

The perfect complement to hot or iced sage tea, this bread treats the taste buds to the rich citrus flavor of lemon balm. Lemon verbena may be substituted for the lemon balm if desired.

INGREDIENTS

1 stick unsalted butter
1/4 cup finely chopped lemon balm leaves
1 cup sugar
2 large eggs
Pinch of salt
1-1/2 cups sifted flour
1 teaspoon baking powder
Grated rind of one lemon
1/4 cup chopped nuts (optional)

GLAZE INGREDIENTS

Juice of 1 lemon
1/2 cup granulated sugar
1/2 cup hot water
1/4 cup finely chopped lemon balm leaves

PROCEDURE

1. Cream butter with lemon balm leaves. Add sugar and beat well. Then add remaining ingredients and mix well.
2. Preheat oven to 350° (178° C). Pour batter into greased loaf pan(s) (1 large, 2 small, or 4 mini). Bake for 30 to 45 minutes, depending upon pan size, or until batter tests done with a toothpick.
3. Mix all glaze ingredients together. After the bread is removed from the oven, pour the glaze over it and allow to sit in the loaf pan(s) for four to six hours.
4. Wrap the bread in foil and allow to ripen overnight before serving or freeze immediately.

MAIL ORDER SOURCES

Plants, seeds, and craft supplies may be ordered by mail from the following companies (**p** = plants; **s** = seeds; **cs** = craft supplies). Please enclose a SASE with your catalog request.

W. Atlee Burpee & Co. (**p, s**)
300 Park Ave.
Warminster, PA 18974

Capriland's Herb Farm (**p, s, cs**)
Silver St.
North Coventry, CT 06238

Carroll Gardens (**p**)
P.O. Box 310
444 East Main St.
Westminster, MD 21157

Hartman's Herb Farm (**p, s**)
Old Dana Rd
Barre, MA 01005

Heirloom Gardens (**p**)
P.O. Box 138
Guerneville, CA 95446

Earl May Seed & Nursery (**p**)
208 N. Elm
Shenandoah, IA 51603

Merry Gardens (**p**)
P.O. Box 595
Camden, ME 04843

Park Seed Co. (**p**)
P.O. Box 46
Greenwood, SC 29647

Pequea Trading Co. (**cs**)
10 East Main Street
Strasburg, PA 17579

Rasland Farm (**p, cs**)
N.C. 82 at U.S. 13
Godwin, NC 28344

Richters (**p, s**)
Goodwood, Ontario LOC 1AD
Canada

Sandy Mush Herb Nursery (**p, s**)
Rt. 2, Surrett Cove Rd.
Leicester, NC 28748

The Sassafrass Hutch (**cs**)
11880 Sandy Bottom, NE
Greenville, MI 48838

Sinking Springs Herb Farm (**p, cs**)
234 Blair Shore Rd.
Elkton, MD 21921

Smile Herb Shop (**cs**)
4908 Berwyn Rd.
College Park, MD 20740

Stillridge Herb Farm (**cs**)
10370 Rt. 99
Woodstock, MD 21163

Tom Thumb Workshops (**cs**)
P.O. Box 322
Chincoteague, VA 23336

Well-Sweep Herb Farm (**p, cs**)
317 Mt. Bethel Rd.
Port Murray, NJ 07865

BIBLIOGRAPHY

Bailey, L.H. *Hortus Third*. New York: Macmillan Publishing Co., 1976.

Barraclough, Daphne. *A Flower-Lover's Miscellany*. London: Frederick Warne & Co., 1961

Bonar, Ann. *The Macmillian Treasury of Herbs*. New York: Macmillan Publishing Co., 1985.

Brownlow, Margaret. *Herbs and the Fragrant Garden*. New York: McGraw-Hill Book Co., 1963.

Bruce, Hal. *How to Grow Wildflowers and Wild Shrubs and Trees in Your Own Garden*. New York: Alfred A. Knopf, 1976.

Clausen, Ruth Rogers, and Nicolas H. Ekstrom. *Perennials for American Gardens*. New York: Random House, 1989.

Coats, Alice M. *Flowers and Their Histories*. New York: Pitman Publishing Co., 1956.

Condon, Geneal. *The Complete Book of Flower Preservation*. Englewood Cliffs, N.J.: Prentice-Hall, 1970.

Crockett, James Underwood, Ogden Tanner, and the editors of Time-Life Books. *Herbs: Time-Life Encyclopedia of Gardening*. Alexandria, Va.: Time-Life Books, 1977.

Dana, Mrs. William. *How to Know the Wild Flowers*. Boston: Houghton Mifflin Co., 1989.

Densmore, Frances. *How Indians Use Wild Plants for Food, Medicine, and Crafts*. New York: Dover, 1974.

Durant, Mary. *Who Named the Daisy? Who Named the Rose? A Roving Dictionary of North American Wildflowers*. New York: Dodd, Mead & Company, 1976.

The Encyclopedia of Organic Gardening. Emmaus, Pa.: Rodale Press, 1972.

Fogg, H.G. Witham. *Dictionary of Annual Plants*. New York: Drake Publishers, 1972

Gallop, Barbara, and Deborah Reich. *The Complete Book of Topiary*. New York: Workman Publishing Co., 1987.

Gordon, Lesley. *A Country Herbal*. New York: Mayflower Books, 1980.

Grieve, Mrs. M. *A Modern Herbal*. New York: Dover Publications, 1971.

Grimm, William Carey. *The Book of Trees*. New York: Harthorn Books, Inc. 1957.

Hausman, Ethel Hinckley. *Beginner's Guide to Wild Flowers*. New York: G.P. Putnam's Sons, 1948.

Hersey, Jean. *The Woman's Day Book of Wildflowers*. New York: Simon and Schuster, 1976.

Hull, Helen S. *Wild Flowers for Your Garden*. New York: M. Barrows & Co., 1952.

Hylton, William H., ed. *The Rodale Herb Book*. Emmaus, Pa.: Rodale Press, 1974.

Klimas, John E., and James A. Cunningham. *Wildflowers of Eastern America*. New York: Galahad Books, 1981.

LeStrange, Richard. *A History of Herbal Plants*. New York: Arco Publishing Co., 1977.

Loewenfeld, Claire. *Herb Gardening: Why and How to Grow Herbs*. Newton, Mass.: Charles T. Branford Co., 1965.

Loewer, Peter, and Anne Meyer. *Secrets of the Great Gardens: How to Make Your Garden as Beautiful as Theirs*. New York: Summit Books, 1991.

Lust, John B. *The Herb Book*. New York: Benedict Lust Publications, 1974.

Martin, Laura C. *Wildflower Folklore*. Charlotte, N.C.: Fast & McMillan Publishers, The Eastwoods Press, 1984.

Miloradovich, Milo. *Growing and Using Herbs and Spices*. New York: Dover Publications, 1952.

New English Dictionary on Historical Principles. Oxford: Clarendon Press, 1901.

Patterson, Allen. *Herbs in the Garden*. London: J.M. Dent & Sons Ltd., 1985.

Pizzetti, Ippolito, and Henry Cocker. *Flowers: A Guide for Your Garden*. Vols. 1–2. New York: Harry N. Abrams, 1975.

Rodale's Illustrated Encyclopedia of Herbs. Emmaus, Pa.: Rodale Press, 1987.

Rose, Jeanne. *Jeanne Rose's Herbal Body Book*. New York: Perigee Books, 1976.

Simmons, Adelma Granier. *Herb Gardening in Five Seasons*. New Jersey: D. Van Nostrand Co., 1980.

Still, Steven M. *Herbaceous Ornamental Plants*. Champaign, Ill.: Stipes Publishing Co., 1980.

Taylor, Norman. *The Guide to Garden Flowers: Their Identity and Culture*. Boston: Houghton Mifflin Co., 1958.

Wilder, Louise Beebe. *The Fragrant Path*. New York: Collier Books, 1990.

METRIC COOKING EQUIVALENTS

1/4 teaspoon	=	1.25 milliliters
1/2 teaspoon	=	2.5 milliliters
1 teaspoon	=	5 milliliters
1 tablespoon	=	15 milliliters
1/4 cup	=	63 milliliters
1/3 cup	=	83 milliliters
1/2 cup	=	125 milliliters
3/4 cup	=	188 milliliters
1 cup	=	250 milliliters
1/2 gallon	=	1.9 liters
1 gallon	=	3.8 liters